W.G & ME

Surviving Wegener's Granulomatosis
(Renamed: Granulomatosis with Polyangiitis)

MAYAR AKASH

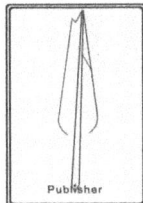

MA PUBLISHER

Mayar Akash

Published by MA Publishing (Penzance)
Published August 2020
ISBN-13: 978-1-910499-32-0

Disclaimer:
The information containing in this book are accounts of the author, no part of this information is professional advice. All readers must do their own diligences and find what is the current guidance for your region of the world? Most of the information in this book is information purpose only, as a way to get direction to seek clarity, alternatives and choices. Please note that the information in the email section was written in 2010 and will be out of date. Please check all links and information for updates on-line. The knowledge about Wegener's Granulomatosis is always being discovered.

Cover designed by Mayar Akash
Typeset in Times New Roman
Copy Edit by Mary Smith

Paper printed on is FSC Certified, lead free, acid free, buffered paper made from wood-based pulp. Our paper meets the ISO 9706 standard for permanent paper. As such, paper will last several hundred years when stored.

Dedication

I dedicate this book to my parents who have nurtured me when they needed nurturing, my father died of lung cancer in 2012 in London. In Bangladesh he was consoling while he was developing cancer and we didn't know then, he looked after me, he was in pain and would tell me but we were none the wiser in Bangladesh.

We lived together with our predicaments, spent some priceless moments and shared our vulnerable and fragile time of our lives with my mother. My mother kept up the morale and looked after both of us. I love you both and may God bless you both.

I would also like to dedicate this book to Bruce who became my beacon, guide when the lights went out in my life, and I fell in to darkness.

Bruce became the person that I latched on after I learnt that I had the rare disease. I could not trust or put faith in professionals, he became the one who I sought guidance from, he was that voice of assurance, the stick of a blind.   I don't know where he is but wherever he is, my prayers, appreciation and gratitude goes out to him.

Dear Bruce,
Thank you, thank you so very much, thank you for becoming my light
Thank you for being my beacon.

A stranger I was, yet with similar inflictions.
I hope you are safe and sound wherever you maybe.
I'm sorry that I am not able to return that which you gave to me.

But, my blessings are yours, my thoughts are yours,
Your light has etched my soul and it still shines within.

I regret that I know not where you are, we were always a world apart
Yet, now you are light within 'til our pass over to thereafter.

Thank you Bruce for being there for me,
When I needed someone - when I was lost, down and on my way out,
Thank you; bless you, love, respect and honour for you.

Acknowledgement

There are many people I need to say thank you to beginning with all my brothers who supported me in both the UK and Bangladesh.

Also, I would like to thank Veronique who was the first person to respond to my SOS. From our communications she helped me to learn which group/disease was affecting me. From Véronique's email, Bruce came into my life and he took over from where she left off. Bruce was a sufferer and he supported the group. Bruce became my source of knowledge and guidance for the disease and I cannot thank him enough. Then there is Cyndi. She also came out of the conversation that I was having in the group. She answered many of my queries along the way, as did Charlotte Stoner and Sue Ashdown from the Oxfordshire Vasculitus Support Group.

In Bangladesh, my 'chaperones' and family members who took care of me and provided me with the protection I needed in this vulnerable stage of my life. My thanks, too, go out to the custodians of Hazrat Shah Jalal's, Mazaar Sharif, Brother Sonnet and his family and to Monir bai's family, Mahbub Rattan bai's family and the hospitality that they had provided me.

Thank you goes out to Rachel (of LBTH), Julie Ann Wheeler and John Dillon for going through the book to help me shape the content in it.

There are many, many more people to thank and my gratitude goes out to them all, all who helped me through ...

Wegener's Granulomatosis.

Love you always and forever
Samir
Amaani
Zainab

Contents

Mayar Akash

*"Nothing but deeds
of our actions
we own and inherit,
that passes on with us"*

Introduction

In December 2009, I was hit with a disease that did not have a cure; one so rare that there is only a chance of 20,000:1of getting it. It was a real 'Wow!' "Timber!" moment in life... it certainly stops you in your tracks. I remember what I call "Twin Peak," moments [Twin Peaks was an American TV programme about strange and mysterious happenings] taking place in my mind - things (imageries) collapsing all around me like a stage change of scenery with colours disappearing into background of grey.

No cure. Knowing that, I began to feel engulfed in doom and gloom. Thoughts of the pain, the dependence I would have on people and my demise, flashed through my mind, slowly materialising, as my dreams, hopes and ideals all ebbed away.

Being such a rare disease meant that I had not heard of it before and neither had anyone in my family or community. There was no-one or any organisation or local specialist that I could turn to.

It was a hard and lonesome journey that I went through, taking small, stumbling steps in the dark, the blackness. However, I was lucky. I found the light and managed to come out the other side ... alive.

This book is all about this journey - sharing my experiences, what I did and how I got to become free of this dreadful disease. I want to provide some light and hope on it so that others can find help, information and guidance before taking giant decisions on medical treatments that may do more harm than good.

I hope there is something for everyone in this book. I know myself, of course, from trawling the web just how much information there is out there –plenty of websites and, in particular, blogs about the disease. However, I could find very few stories in books about individual sufferers.

I am not sure how my book is going to be received. Having read many of the stories in the 'yahoo' groups and so on, as well as the fact that many of the sufferers who had supported me had been suffering for decades, will probably make this book seem like a walk in the park compared to what they have had to go through.

A walk in the park, it was not. The trauma was very real and immense; the medical challenges for me were completely daunting; just as any new environment or entity can be. This book is about me looking back at the circumstances I found myself in; attempting to unpick where and how the healing may have taken place.

It is my survival story.

Life

My life has had so many 'ups and downs' which have tested me emotionally, mentally and spiritually. From an early age I sustained these challenges that were continually shaping me even though I could not understand why these things were happening to me - my continual internal questioning. I suffered many metaphorical car crashes in my life and an actual one. This one left me with misaligned vertebrae and post-traumatic stress for well over a decade.

I actually felt that I was a simple and straightforward person and really quite 'low maintenance' but contrary to this belief, people and family around me found me difficult as I did not fit into their status quo.

So I made my choices and lived my life. Unfortunately, this did not go according to how I had planned or imagined it would be, much of it was due to my naivety and inexperience.

After my first divorce, for months I hid away and remained low key. I felt as if I had HIV Aids and it was written on my forehead for all to see. I felt very self-conscious and remember one day walking through Whitechapel market on my way to work and feeling uncomfortable walking in the crowd; even though these people were from all walks of life who did not know me and maybe just a few that did.

This anxiety took a while to subside. However, my anxiety was not active on the outside but in my psyche. I started burying myself in my work and distracted myself as much as I could. I slowly began to find my bearings and could concentrate on my business again and also focused spending time with a couple of school friends.

After a year or so I found myself, as the saying goes, "out of the frying pan and in to the fire," - my friends set me up with someone who would go on to be my second wife. It all happened pretty quickly [too quickly] with one thing leading to another and soon there was talk of marriage.

Unfortunately, the marriage took a turn for the worse and eventually, after eight years of ups and downs, ended with an estrangement when I fell ill with the disease. I was on my own, desperately trying to make sense of my life. I was not seeing anyone, nor was I involved in any sexual activities. I was in a state of complete introspection, in my 'man cave' - totally alone. I did not want to burden any members of my family, particularly my parents who were both in Bangladesh at this time.

Turmoils

It was really rough and there's nothing like the 'warm bed' I had left behind. However, I had to deal with it. I was on a roller coaster ride of emotional and mental turmoil.

I was now going through my second divorce and had so many practical worries - getting a place to stay, avoiding contact, re-planning my life, re-shaping my world, dealing with the pain of separation, what strategies to use to deal with the loneliness, how to entertain myself, what to eat, how to make the money last, what kind of a person was I? What kind of father was I? Putting yet another child of mine through this, what was I going to tell the family? That I did not want to speak or see the in-laws, resentment towards the estranged wife, resentment towards the in-laws, resentment towards my life, and resentment towards myself and how I handled things. I was having highs and lows.

I had not been able to get all my belongings but had some - a sleeping bag, a few clothes, my laptop and cameras, so that at least gave me some peace of mind.

In my mind, I resented how she [my wife] treated me. I resented how she spoke to me in front of the children, how belittled I felt, how she shamed me. I felt very much as though I was being treated like a dog in front of my own child and this was something that I did not want to endure for the rest of my life. It became the reason for me leaving.

I did not want to be subjected to it, nor did I want my child to witness it. More to the case, I did not want to be in front of her when it took place.

I did not know how to handle these situations as I was not equipped to do so. I did not want to 'rise to the bait' in these situations and incidents, so I was left feeling demoralised, having no self-worth or value and wondering how my life had reached such a low level.

Forgetting

With all the things that were going on which I was not capable of dealing with, I started forgetting things but continued living in my 'bubble' and was just getting by. For me there were so many internal relationship issues that were eating me up -I was no good for me and I was certainly no good for my child in the environment and atmosphere I was living in.

I had so many issues to sort out. I had nowhere to stay and I was determined that I was not going to burden any of my family members in this country and my parents were back home in Bangladesh. Most of my belongings I had left behind, I did not have a car at that time.

I had to make plans to sleep somewhere. I did have access to my brother's shop as I was a key holder and I stayed there for couple of weeks.

Also at this time, I was working in Newham and was a key holder to the office. It was a couple days to the Christmas break and the office was going to be closed for that period, so I moved into the basement where I made a space on the floor to sleep - fully dressed in my sleeping bag on the settee cushions laid out on the floor.

I was not in contact with anyone but I was accessible on my mobile phone.

It was snowing outside and cold. The basement was very cold and although there was heating available, I was conscious not to abuse the use of the electricity but I was concerned as the cold and damp aggravated my asthma, as did breathing in dust when sleeping on the tile-carpeted floor.

Train of chained thoughts

My mind was locked in a constant chain of thoughts that kept looping around again and again. The scolding, that I was 'worst of the worst', that I was 'pathetic'...I was experiencing the peeling off of me as a person, a human being, layers of self-worth and belief. These emotions were constantly streaming through my head and mind with my heart churning from leaving another child of mine. However, in this present state, I was no good to anyone.

The hostility of the relationship, the circumstances of the estrangement, the abandonment of yet another child, divorce and still the turmoil of the first one, all fought for a place in my head and, of course, what about the public perception of me [people who knew me]; my family's perception of me; my children's perception of me?

I was having intense bouts of highs and lows, from melancholy to tearfulness and crying, when I reached the level where I felt completely useless and unloved, projecting how I wanted my life to be, as I saw in my mind's eye how other typical young families behaved, played, laughed and happily interacted.

What was I going to do now? What about tomorrow? Next month? Next year? Knowing that I could not stay estranged from the impending separation and divorce news for ever but feeling that I could not face it.

I think my first marriage separation and divorce took me to the extreme but this time round pushed me well beyond my capabilities and capacity to cope. I reached the 'edge' far more quickly, suffering severe bouts of pain and anguish, self-doubt, and torment. I dwelt on the judgements that would be going on -how did people perceive me, what did my family think, what did the 'in-laws' think, what my children thought; and further anxiety about what the 'ex' in-laws would think. All this stemmed from my past experiences. I had already had comments that I was incapable of keeping down a relationship and that there was something wrong with me because of this happening a second time. How was I going to be able to deal with this? How long would it take to overcome the various stages: emotional, mental, spiritual, social and personal?

My autonomous side was also in auto-protective mode and was attempting to process a myriad of thoughts. How to cleanse myself, review, re-evaluate, re-assess, negotiate, re-negotiate, wail, lament, detached - emotional, memories, thoughts, sounds, smells, expressions, sights, physiological pain and residual thoughts, feelings, physical contacts, notions of the 'fuck ups', what I did and did not do, stand my ground, why didn't I say 'this or that,' when this happened or that happened; playing in the head; discovering where I should have taken action but did not, adopting the policy to find the good in a bad situation/circumstance to stay; being over powered, falling victim to criticism and scolding, becoming a door mat; living and moving into the 'Mrs's' place, getting into debt, being in debt, making plans to pay child maintenance contributions, finding a way of sealing the chance of not going back, thinking about going abroad, how it was repeating for the second time in my life, why was it repeating again, what was wrong with me, preventing myself falling into depression, melancholy, mood swings, killing time, no one to talk to; alone, lonely, recollecting, recalling, broken record –the 'highs' of my life and the 'lows'; protecting myself, preserving myself.

I'm free, I'm lost and I'm low: comfort eating, junk-food eating and drinking, chicken and chips, spreading the cost, budgeting £2 per day. Hate, anger, despair, frustration, hurt, pain, disappointments, sadness, sorrow, pity, feeling sorry for myself -all these different states of mind! What else would happen to an introspective person such as me?

Out on my own

So while in that state of mind, isolated, lonely no one to talk to, cold and damp in a basement of an office building with desks, books, computers and filing cabinets surrounding me, I induced myself to go into my thoughts, into my mind. I could not see any 'light at the end of the tunnel' or in my mind's eye.

I was trying to keep myself busy, to distract myself from slipping into deep depression, so I spent lots of time on the laptop watching 'you tube' clips and listening to songs.

It was Christmas week and cold and snowing outside and very few people about. I would only pop upstairs to go to the toilet and then come straight back down so that no one could see me from outside. I was, in effect, hiding there so that was adding just another mental pressure.

I had the sniffles and was wheezy; I was trying to stay warm wearing a thick arctic jacket whilst wrapped in a sleeping bag. I was also trying to write 'stuff' in a note pad. Thoughts had to be written down in order to alleviate them and lighten my mind - typing them directly on to the laptop did not help. I also had books to read and some work to get on with which I attempted to do.

Meditation

I was alone and trying to do all sorts of things and one of them was that I was going to meditate. I wanted to get my inner-self to help me improve my immune system. I was breathing deeply in through my nose and out through my mouth. While I was breathing, in my mind I was talking to myself, telling myself to clean my blood and improve my immune system so that I would not fall ill and be in better health.

So, from the sniffle I began getting pain in the back of my left eye which I thought was being caused by the cold creeping up on me. In the beginning, I tried not to take any painkillers because I had used paracetamol in the past and had become tolerant to around eight to ten tablets a day and this got higher and higher but then I completely stopped.

Pain

The pain became more and more uncomfortable with a hot burning sensation in the socket area. I then started taking *'Solpadine Max,'* to alleviate the pain, which helped but the discomfort continued to get worse and worse. It got to the point where I could not move my left eye to look from side to side, I could move my eyeball but it was horrendously painful, excruciating. I was in great pain. I had a temperature, my eye was so sore, heavy and burning- the heat was permeating around my eye socket to the back of my head.

Loss of sight

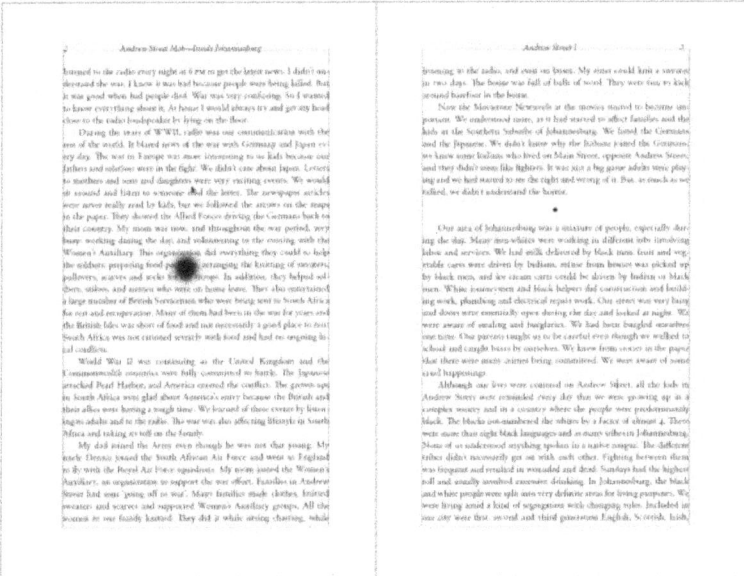

To look around I had to move my whole head making sure that the eyeball did not move. Again, I took two more Solpadine Max and the pain subsided a bit. Later in the afternoon, I sat down and picked up a book to read but when I opened it to the page I wanted to read, I noticed a black patch and I could not see the letters in that section of my vision. In a matter of milliseconds I tried to focus but the blank bit was still there. I didn't wait or hesitate but immediately made my way to the Royal London Hospital's Walk-In Centre. I think it was the 24[th]December and the A&E was closed.

I waited for hours and was finally seen by a supply nurse who had a quick look and discharged me with conjunctivitis. She said that if I was not happy then I was to go to the Moorfields Eye Hospital - which I did.

Moorfields

I went to the Moorfields A&E and was seen by a doctor who discharged me with two eye drops, one for each eye. I was not impressed with this either as it did not help alleviate the symptoms or the pain. However, the doctor had said to come back for a review on the following Wednesday.

So, I continued to use the eye drops and take the pain killers but the soreness of the eye was not reducing and I was still suffering. I continued to stay in the office. When the Wednesday came, I attended the review clinic and further tests were carried out but the doctor could not come to any conclusions so he sent me for an ultrasound scan.

The ultrasound scan and then the taking of a picture of the eye showed a flare-up of a small vein in the back of the eyeball. It was at this point that I was sent for many different tests, one of which was an Anti Neutrophils Cytoplasmic Antibody (ANCA) blood test.

The following week, I was referred to Professor Sue Lightman's clinic where the ANCA results came back positive. The consultant asked me if I had been scratched by a cat because the symptoms were similar to a disease related to this sort of scratch and mentioned that it was like Wegener's Granulomatosis but this needed further investigations before it could be confirmed. So, another batch of blood was taken for testing but because that day was a public holiday, the pharmacy was closed so no medicine was given and I was sent home with another appointment to come back.

I felt dismissed, until the next appointment. I was so depressed and felt vulnerable and fragile. It broke me even further when they let me go home without any medicine. I was dreading having to endure the pain during my wait. I was later to learn that, inadvertently, this period also allowed the virus to continue to do further damage to me.

The fact that I had to endure further pain really annoyed me and resentment started to grow straight away. I was pain-ridden and had to take over-the-counter painkillers to manage the pain and the high temperature. Reflecting back, when I did go back for the following check-ups, I was prescribed 60mg of Prednisalone and Omeprazole. I was given instructions about Prednisalone and I how it was prescribed for me to 'taper' it down. At this point I still had no diagnosis. However, I could see what difference the medicine made. The swelling and the pain went down and it gave me pain relief.

So during the following visits I was diagnosed. I was told that I had Wegener Granulomatosis (WG) and that I was having the text book symptoms. I later found out that they had not written any notes of the disease in my file. The trainee consultant explained that it is a vasculitus disease which affects the small veins of the upper body. It is an auto-immune disorder, where your own immune system turns on itself and starts attacking you. It is a rare disease and there is no cure.

"Had I known about my blood type and group then, I would have made some life choices that would have avoided many pitfalls."

As soon as I knew the diagnosis, it triggered my inquisitive side, and my need to know more just grew. I was good with computers and soon 'Googled,' it but I was not ready to deal with the information that was out there. There was plenty of it but nothing conclusive. The more I read, the deeper I got, it was like watching the quick-sand scenario - the more you moved, the more you sank.

The bottom line was that there was no cure and the disease was still being researched. No cure and a survival rate of between four to five years. There were no specialist hospitals but three research facilities, one in Hammersmith hospital in London and the others in Birmingham and Cambridge.

I had so many questions about the information I had found. There was plenty of research material but very little guidance. I did not find any peace or comfort in opening this Pandora's Box. My anxiety just grew.

I went to Moorfield's Eye Hospital for a review. It started off with routine checks and then the doctor did a further test just to be thorough.

I had another ultrasound scan done of the eye and further pictures were taken of the veins at the back of the eye.

So, having been seen by various trainee consultants at the Moorfields Eye Hospital my next stage was to go to one of the three specialist research clinics, one being in Hammersmith, London where I would be checked and tested. I did not like the idea of that at all - becoming a guinea pig and a Bangladeshi guinea pig at that.

Before my next appointment when I would be referred to the research facility, I would get an air flight and leave for Bangladesh - to my parents. I could not accept that I was going to be a human guinea pig or the likelihood of having to take strong medicines and/or submit to trial and error therapies.

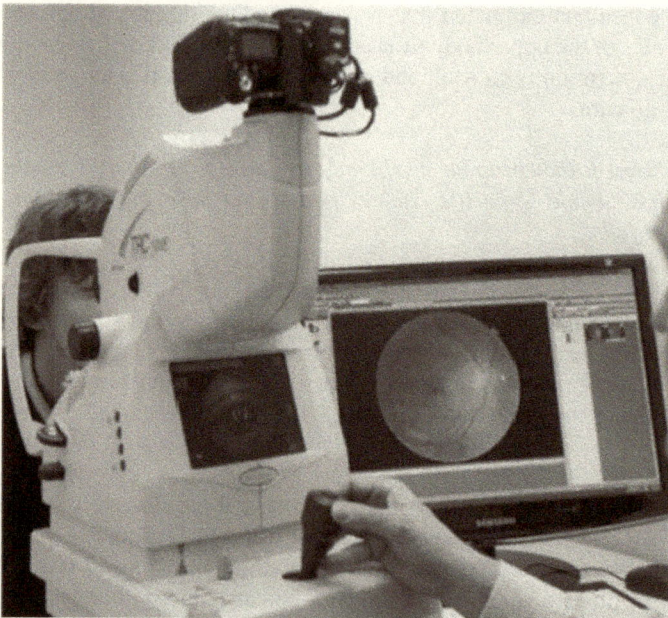

Image captured from Google search

After Diagnosis

OMG! So many things were going through my head. I thought about what I had so far done and achieved? What about my children? What was I supposed to do? I had to let go of the emotional ties and harden up. I needed to unload the pain and the weakness. I could not be there for them and they could not be here for me. I had nothing to show or call my own.

During this sombre time, I had no wife and no children, not because of their choice but because of my own actions to my reaction. No house or home to call my own - nothing in my name, nothing in my life and world. All this just added to my sadness and depression. They became layers in my mind, hundreds and hundreds of layers building in my heart, mind, thoughts and sighs. I was overwhelmed, implosion after implosion that simply pushed me past my mental 'safe' zone.

This was really a humbling moment. I was at a level where reality checked on me. It was just me. No partner, no children, no home, no house, no rights but duty bound in my brother's house. I was becoming a burden.

I was a fish out of water and a human in space without the air. There had been no warning signs for the disease and if there had been, I surely had not known or understood it. It had come on hard and strong and came to do harm … and it did.

"Who set the alien within free in me"

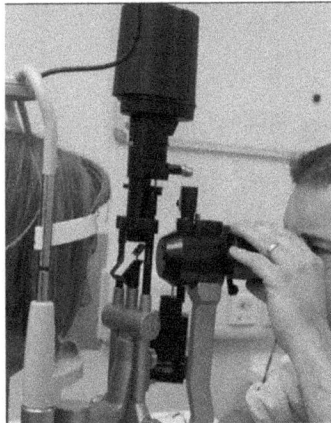

Image captured from Google search

I informed my older brother about the diagnosis and told him that I had Wegener's Granulomatosis (WG) and I was still staying in the office as the offices were still closed; as there was work being done on the shop floor.

I was taking the Prednisalone and I was changing, physically and in appearance, as well as my sleep pattern. I was on the laptop 'Googling' as much information about the illness as I could while the pain in the eye stabilised. I found myself weak and my joints were aching and I was looking dishevelled. I was not sleeping well and I could not even carry a carrier bag, my joints started hurting.

After couple of days, I got a call from my older brother who asked me to come over to his house. I moved in and was there for a week or so. I was sleeping on the settee and continuing to research about the disease. I started searching for help. I found groups on yahoo and started signing up. I sent out an 'SOS' email to a group for help and guidance.

This was such lonesome time in my life trying to confront this incurable disease with a life expectancy of only four to five years.

Everything was altering, my life had completely changed and I was in the wilderness on my own.

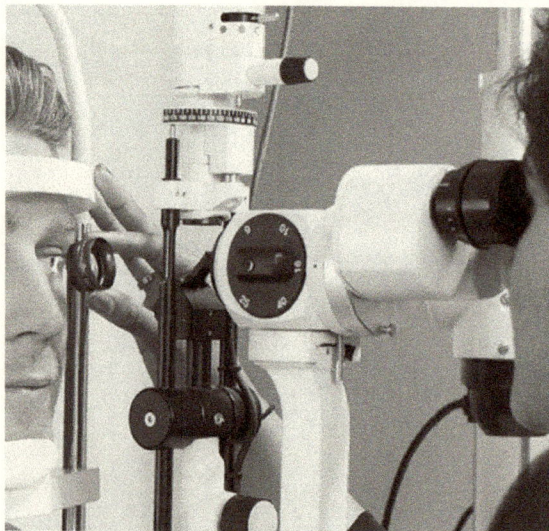
Image captured from Google search

I was heavily researching and as I learned more and more, so many things were happening and I was physically deteriorating. I could not see it but the family did and they, too, could not make sense of the disease.

As a last resort, my brother just said to go to mum and dad - at least there they could offer some comfort.

I was there in the presence of my brother's family but they did not know or understand what I was going through. I could not speak it or ask them questions, just ended up asking God. Why? That, too, was not going to help. I was being pulled deeper and deeper into this subject, falling but there was no-one to catch me.

"Even at this point, I was not clear on what the diagnosis was. I described the symptoms to the yahoo group and the response I got back from them clarified for me as to what was wrong with me."

I learnt that I had a rare disease. There was a 20,000:1 chance of getting it. It usually happens to people over the age of forty but there I was, still in my late thirties! It also confirmed that it was still in its research stage, so there was still no cure and there were only a certain number of years to live – a survival rate of between three to five years.

This disease would damage me in an irrecoverable way. It starts with the left eye, then the right and then works its way down through the body. Learning this stirred up terrible emotion inside me as new thoughts began to flood in. Wow, I have not lived and whatever life I had lived had not been fulfilling, misspent time and many other inhibitions began to surface.

As I was taking the Prednisalone, many things were beginning to happen to me. I was not sleeping well, getting depressed and withdrawn, I was starting to feel weaker within myself and more fatigued; tired and aching - joints hurting. I could only just about walk but I could not carry anything.

This triggered so many thoughts about how I used to tell my mum to exercise to make her muscles stronger, and this now made me feel so bad. I was sorry that I had done that because of the way that I was feeling, even though I was a still a young person. My vision was becoming blurred and I had a slight hearing reduction in the left ear, as well as intermittent hearing blanks.

Immune system
I was down and out and not in a very good place. I continued to self-question, analyse, interrogate, counsel and reason with myself. I could not believe that my own immune system had turned on itself, turned on me - was attacking me, the system was working to kill the body, the person, the human.

I was in such a state of self-disbelief.

"Bloody hell–with an illness like this, who needs enemies? It works in the same way as cancer - the cells start attacking themselves."

I meditated and focussed my mind to tell the body to improve my immune system - to clean the blood and get rid of any foreign bodies. I retraced and replayed this back in my mind again and again.

I could not believe it nor could I understand that my own immune system was attacking me for!

Had I known then about my blood group and what it means for me, I would have managed myself better than I did. My blood group 'O' is prone to having auto-immune disorders. It is highly sensitive and defined and has only a small margin of 'give' and error.

The blood type you are also sets out your life, what best to eat, how to be, and your ideal occupation in life and so on. This knowledge about blood types has been around for a while and much of it is supported by scientific evidence. In fact, this information is widely used in Japan for much of the social living.

There is abundant information about this on the web and I have also made references to some books later, on page 127.

Alone

I remember being told by the trainee fellow consultant that I have Wegener's Granulomatosis. I was on my own when I was told, I didn't know what to think and how to feel. The information given to me at that moment was unclear to me but the following things remain etched in my mind:

- Wegener's Granulomatosis!
- It is a vasculitus disease
- This disease solidifies the small veins, thus causing ruptures in the organs.
- It is a rare disease
- There is no cure for it.

When I got back to where I was staying, I immediately searched for this on-line. What I discovered just crystallised me, I froze.

…The immune system turns on itself - the immune system starts attacking its self - my inside was attacking my body and, effectively, wanted to kill it.

This disease is brought on by depression.

In learning this, my whole world just shrank; all dreams and aspirations just popped! Simply in a moment, it disappeared.

The immediate environment I was in, was a lonely place, I wasn't with or around anyone.

With no-one to share my news, nor to turn to for support, I bottled it for weeks. I was just about managing the days and nights and felt numb, shelving all the long term plans, starting to offload immediate plans, physically shedding material objects and attachments such as clothes and books; holding on to the basics - electronics, my phone, laptop and the debit card.

All hopes of being someone or being rich or famous were wiped up, being a father, a husband, a good person or even a bad person all fizzled away.

The attitude of work hard and play later became irrelevant as my life span shortened to just a few years.

The thought of my health deteriorating just took over. I did not understand what was happening to me at that stage but reflecting back, my body was internally preparing, my internal defence mechanism was getting ready for the days to come.

All I remember was that I was mentally preparing for pain management – I was enquiring, contemplating, anticipating what kind of pain I would be enduring and the level of pain against my physical self; how weak I would be and how much deterioration would take place with each bout.

I felt resigned to the fact that I was going to die, but although I was resigned, I was not ready to die, fully. My human self was not ready to die and this became apparent later on. This thought was very painful on top of the numbness of learning I was dying.

The numbness was like suspension, suspended in the air, hanging!
- My life!
- What about my life?
- How long was my life?
-.How short is my life?
-.What have I lived?

Reflecting back, it was like the force of a tsunami inside of me – mentally and emotionally; thoughts and recollections were chasing through my head. I had so many vivid memories which seemed to free-fall in and out of my mind - my dad's stroke and his suffering, one of my uncles dying from stomach cancer and how emaciated and yellow he was; his deterioration to death; then my brother's wife's brother, who I had loved as a brother with infectious jolly personality, who died of stomach cancer, too, in America when the twin towers were still standing. When I had gone to see him in hospital - he had all sorts of machines to support him: respiratory ventilator, kidney dialysis, pipes draining his urine, air pumps on his legs to circulate the flow of blood and all the gadgets monitoring his vital signs; the distress, the pain, the dependency and so on. My mind was doing over-time.

Reaching out

After being told that I had a rare disease called Wegener's Granulomatosis, which had no cure, my immediate thought reaction was that I was going be lab rat and then die.

This became a very dark period of my life.

I was prescribed Prednisalone, steroids which were taking their toll on me and they were feeding my implosion of feelings.

Having joined the groups in yahoo, replies started coming back and I began to establish a base for myself. Talking to people who were going through it and who had years of experience helped to shed some light on the matter and my sombre mood. To learn that I was not alone in the world helped but I was the only Bangladeshi on the system and the majority of the sufferers were from America.

I made enquiries about sufferers in Britain and also what support was out there for me. There were only a few sufferers in the UK but there were facilities being set up and an organisation in Oxford.

In this section, I have captured my email communications. I was throwing myself out there for help, guidance, clarifications and people to talk to who knew about this disease.

Shot in the dark!

The intended purpose for inclusion of these emails is to give the reader a first-hand account of what happened to me and how I proceeded when there was no information or group readily available to help me in the United Kingdom in 2010.

NB: the following email conversations you are about to read are the actual email communications I had, in which I was told that I had Wegener's Granulomatosis. The information that is contained in the emails is for information purposes, the emails are in their entirety. Please check information and links with officials and verified sites.

The emails are in date order and are my correspondence with more than one person.

Sent email: 1

Hi, I am an individual. I was told today that I have Wagner but this will be confirmed in 4 weeks from today, awaiting the 2nd blood ANCA test.

It is daunting to read about this. It is also daunting that there was no warning, beforehand, then again I'm not sure as I look into this, things may flag up from the past, which was a tell-tale sign anyway, I'm entering into something on my own, so it's unclear how to proceed.

I not sure what this means for the future, what should I be preparing for, some of the research has spooked me.

M

(Thursday 28th January 2010 *In wagnersyndrome@ yahoogroups. com, "mayarakash" <mayarakash@ wrote* ☺)

The lifeline I got back were the following emails:

Received email: 1

Hi M

I think you mean: Wegener Granulomatosis. Sometimes the patient doesn't understand the doctor correctly. Wagner syndrome is ocular only. Wegener Granulomatosis is an auto-immune disease that can have devastating effects. For more information<u>http://www.vasculit is foundation.</u>
<u>*org/wegenersgranulomatosis*</u>

Take care, Veronique

(From: Veronique Nas <nasveronique@yahoo.com>, To: wagnersyndrome@yahoogroups.com, Sent: Thu, January 28, 2010 7:53:30 AM, Subject: [wagnersyndrome] Re: Wagner families in the UK)

After receiving Veronique's reply back I felt more grounded, however, I was still in the dark and had many miles to go to understanding what I had been diagnosed with. So, on Friday 29th January 2010, I then sent her my long email as follows on the next page.

Sent email: 2

Hi Veronique,

Thank you for your email. It has been helpful, The information and some of the patients stories have settled me a bit on one hand and increased my tenacity to learn more.

As of yet I don't exactly know what it is that I have, I will be seeing my GP [on the] coming Monday.

Now that I am facing this, I've been reflecting on what I have experienced past and present.

This particular problem came within 7-10 days. I initially experienced tenderness behind my eye ball, the pain then started to increase; this I didn't take it too seriously as I was able to handle the nagging pain.

[A] Few days after the onset of the pain, I picked up a book to read and immediately saw a blur in the left eye, part of the vision was blurred, This is when I got alarmed and went to my Local hospital "walk in centre", after waiting 3 hours the A&E spent max ten minutes and discharged me with "conjunctivitis" and gave me a reason for the blur to be "watery eyes", I didn't accept that and told him that I know what a watery eye blur is like, you can wipe away the tears, he then told me that if I wasn't happy to go to Moorfields eye hospital.

I went to Moorfields eye hospital and after standard test I was discharged with the same diagnosis and with 2 eye drops and an ointment, but was told to come in for a review in couple of day's time.

Even at the review the doctor was unable to diagnose WG and had the inkling that he might have overlooked something, he then got me to have ultrasound scan of the eye.

The ultra scan picked up inflammation in the middle of my eye ball; this explained the blur that I had. After that I had the eye ball photographed, dye injection to type, the red ray test, the blue ray test, a blood test and a couple others which photographed the eye but not MRI.

The vein at the back of the eye was inflamed and pink, the inflammation was visible and it was white in colour, behind a grey translucent inflammation.

Before being prescribed Prednisalone I had a throbbing pain in the eye ball, the eye socket and half of head and skull on the left side.

Unfortunately for me, I went in to Moorfield's where the ultrasound picked up the inflammation but it was 2 days before New Year's day, and the clinic was half day, so I was sent home without anything and told to continue using the drops, using the drops was pointless. So for the next seven days the pain grew worse and worse and [I] had to resort to pain killers. I was taking 2x500mg paracetamol and codeine. My eyeball was red, watering and hot and sore.

I am now in Professor Lightman's clinic in Moorfields Eye Hospital, London. Professor Lightman is overseeing my case.

Looking back, I have had a number of medical issues.

I have asthma and mild psoriasis to my knee caps and elbows.

I had an accident when I sustained a head injury to the back of my head, and as a result I suffered from cold and flu with runny nose for about ten years, when I learned to manage the problems. What I recall was that I was not able to regulate my body temperature, when I was cold I used to wear jumpers and jacket and when I was hot I did the same because I felt cold. So in the cold I would wear a lot of clothes and then sweat and feel cold and summer I would sweat and feel cold and wear clothes,

I generally sweat heavily during physical activities, as if I have had a shower - at times I can feel the sweat just popping out of my head.

When I joined my new GP I told him and also was in my records that near enough I was getting bronchitis on [a] regular and yearly basis, he said this was uncommon for a young person, so he sent me to have and x ray of the chest. The x-ray showed I had a lesion in my right lung. He then sent me for an MRI and that came with more details, I was then referred to see the consultant, his name I cannot remember, [who]discharged me saying it was nothing to worry about. As if, if it's there, it got there somehow?

My right lung has always been the ticklish when I got infections or a cough if I touched a cotton bud on my right eye, it will directly tickle in my right lung and make me cough. Also during coughs, cold and bronchitis, if I slept on my right side, my lungs would be uncomfortable, and I would cough and be in pain but then if I flipped over and slept on the left side then I would be comfortable. I have had problems with my eye lid, blocked tear glands and itchy eye.

I am aware that my immune system is not strong.

I also suffered for ten years as a result of the accident, because the spinal nerve was trapped, and limited the flow for ten years. When the physiotherapist freed up the spinal cord in my spinal column I experienced an immediate rush to my head and that night, I had a deep sleep.

I have also for much of my life had issues with depression, emotional problems, stress and anxiety and also expect a lot out of myself. The head injury also left me with "lack of spatial awareness", losing balance when standing and when drinking from a can or bottle or even a cup, one out five times, it will spill off the side of my lips; forgetfulness - these [things] very minor but I've been monitoring myself when I realised that this was happening and I didn't understand why I kept on doing it.

Thanks I just wanted to get it out of my system. Maybe there is a clue as to the triggers, I wonder if the people who suffer ever had a head injury, or breathed in asbestos or other agents that we learn years later, as part of some experiment.
Look forward to your reply.
Thanks

Mayar Akash

This moment, in my life, time had become constricted, like an egg timer, where once it was like standing on a sand dune on a coastal beach and taking a deep breath and watching the vastness of time, to then it shrinking to an egg timer and watching it flow out downwardly. I was numb, from learning my diagnosis and then to double that, I was under steroid medication that was adding to my dishevelledness from within. I continued 'Googling' for more information, as an introspective person my brain was working overtime - the thoughts, anxiety, stress, bewilderment, the prospect of being no more, claustrophobia then set in. Painfully for my brother, it was visible on the outside but there was very little comfort he was able to offer me. I am certain that he was doing his own research on this subject matter.

There was no-one there for me who could settle me, reassure me as there were no known specialist fully-funded groups, whether paid or voluntary. However, there were groups on-line that I discovered - there was a little light in the dark.

I was grounded again when I received Veronique's reply and I drank in what she had to say, as if I was quenching my thirst.

Received email: 2

Hi Mayar

From what you are writing I would say you definitely have Wegener Granulomatosis and not Wagner syndrome. Is this professor Lightman an ophthalmologist? Moorefield's is of course an excellent eye clinic, but maybe you should go to a specialist on WG as well.

On yahoo there are several groups discussing WG. If you put Wegener Granulomatosis in the "Search for other groups..." box, you will find at least three.
Take care!
Véronique.

(From: Veronique Nas <nasveronique@yahoo.com, To: wagnersyndrome@yahoogroups.com, Sent: Fri, January 29, 2010 8:52:35 AM, Subject: [wagnersyndrome] Re: Wagner families in the UK)

This email from Veronique made me focus on what I had and that there should be no more confusion. I recollected what the consultant told me but after leaving the clinic but I had lost the thread and got tangled in the wordings of "Wagners & Wegeners". This was a good intervention which saved me unnecessary anxiety and being in a continued state of confusion searching for both diseases. I calmed myself down -okay, we are getting clearer, one less worry to deal with.

Nevertheless, what the email did not do is take me by the hand and give me the reassurance that I had found a place where I could get some guidance. I replied back to Veronique and followed her sign posting.

Sent email: 3

Hi Veronique,

I will certainly search for the other groups. You know at this point in time the question in the back of my mind was, how long is my future, how should I prepare or position myself.

Thanks M

So after the emailing Veronique I started messaging in the groups that came up from the searches over the next couple of days and received a welcome message from the WGdiscussion group on Yahoo. I then emailed Cyndi with thanks and my concerns on the 1st of February 2010. The 1st February was a very good day for me, it is the date I received my light.

Sent email: 4

Hi Cyndi,

Thank you for the welcome.

I have been recently told that I have the WG and I was prescribed on 60mg of Prednisalone, this is now being reduced as the inflammation in the eye is reducing, the blur in the left eye only, the blurred vision has come down, but the blur is still obstructing me.

I am now experiencing burping and muscle aches, and at times my knees and joints clicking, I am taking cod liver oil for that. I have read some of the sites and am concerned about osteoporosis and the kidney problems.

Also the fact that once one eye recovered then the other eye starts.
I am anxious to learn what precautionary measures I can take to limit or prevent some of those problems;

What is the group's position on taking, grape seed & Echinacea, thistle milk & dandelion roots.

Thanks, Mayar Akash

Though I was making grounds with reaching out to the web groups, I was swimming in the ocean of the internet and the information in it is vast, raw and bitter.

Having access to all this information was great but if you do not have the basic knowledge, it is useless and dangerous if you start experimenting. As a pragmatic person what was I going to do? I pursued all angles available to me. I was visiting the clinic, so while my health deteriorated, I know I was looking dishevelled and gaunt around my face. I was not looking after my hygiene, was not shaving but spent my time sitting behind the laptop, searching and reading. I was also getting weaker. I was having severe joint pain and had difficulty carrying carrier bags with light shopping, which, considering I used to carry two to three bags with groceries in for the family in both hands…

Received email: 3

I received this message from Cindy.

"Stay away from Echinacea, it boosts the immune system
which is the exact opposite of our goal. Our immune systems
are already over-active, we don't want to exacerbate the
problem.

Grapefruit seed extract, I use in many forms, and I sing it's
praises. But anyone taking CTX may want to stay away from it
as grapefruit is a no-no while on CTX.

Have you checked the food lists in the Files section of this site?
Cyndi "

(From: cyndingary <cyndingary@yahoo.com, To: wgdiscussion@yahoogroups.com, Sent: Mon, February 1, 2010 10:41:56
PM, Subject: [wgdiscussion] Re: Welcome to the group / Mayar)

While I was using my own conventional knowledge very limited
things just as vitamins, minerals and herbal. I still needed to connect
with some who knew the illness well and Cindy was well versed in
that disease and the alternatives.

During this time another member of the group replied to me, who went on to
become my light, my beacon and the one hand I held. He was a sufferer as
most of the people in the group were. I received the following email that shed
some more light into my life and world.

Received email: 4

"Hello, Mayar..

If you have WG, then this is a good place to be and you're welcome among the several hundred patients and caregivers with lots of knowledge, experience and support.

Good to hear your one eye is better and I hope the other eye responds well to treatment. Long term use of prednisone can cause cataracts. Fortunately it doesn't always, and cataract surgery is a routine out-patient procedure with excellent results should you develop cataracts.

I wonder where you are as there aren't good vasculitus physicians everywhere.

The most important thing you can do is to be treated by an expert in vasculitus. There aren't many outside major medical centres and teaching hospitals, and only a few of those. Your current physician can consult at no cost with any of the consultants to the Vasculitus Foundation listed at http://www.vasculitisfoundation.org/node/44

Generally speaking, prednisone alone won't keep WG in a long term quiet condition (remission). Usually it takes an immunosuppressive such as Cytoxan, Cellcept, Imuran, etc. along with the prednisone.

For crisis situations, there's multiple treatments of plasmapheresis or of intravenous immunoglobulin G (IVIg). If all else fails, Rituximab has been remarkable successful in treating recalcitrant WG. Both Rituximab and IVIg are very expensive. None of the treatments are risk free, but untreated WG is generally fatal within two years.

Generally, patients on prednisone (or similar glucocorticoids) are put on supplements calcium (1200-1500 mg/day), extra vitamin D3 (400-1000 I.U./day) and a bone loss prevention medication such as Fosamax or PTH. If you're not taking any of those, ask your physician about the need to prevent bone loss. Weight bearing exercise can help prevent bone loss, however prednisone weakens muscles and tendons, so exercise must be moderate. Ask your physician about exercise limits.

Muscle aches and roving joint pains are rather common with WG and similar conditions. Usually with effective treatment, those symptoms will improve and usually disappear.

Below is a long message I send to those newly joining a WG group. I hope it's useful to you. I have NO medical training, so nothing I say should be taken to be medical advice. Refer all medical symptoms, questions, problems, and concerns to appropriate licensed medical professionals.

Best wishes for your early improvement and long lasting remission of the WG".

Bruce (WG '97)

100.com, Sent: Mon, February 1, 2010 10:03:11 PM,
Subject: Re: [wgdiscussion] Re: Welcome to the group (was no subject))

Wow, this was the guidance I needed and looking for and Bruce certainly captured me. So I started to reply back to him straight away into the early hours of the morning of Tuesday 2nd of February 2010.

Sent email: 5

Thank you Bruce;

This is the kind of information I need to start understanding where I am now in life and what it is that I have.

I live in London, England, United Kingdom.

I must say having read this email, the way my GP has been talking, he is telling me "tough luck" you have to deal with it.

I am now more concerned that a recent x ray didn't show any signs, and the report came back normal. However, [a] couple of years ago I had an x ray and a lesion showed up which was followed with a CT scan and that too confirmed the lesion but the consultant discharged me saying it was nothing, this did not give me much confidence in the information given, but [I] did not pursue a second opinion. What I can say that whenever I have had flu or coughs and bronchitis the right lung was always irritating, tickling when breathing or inhaling to cough; this in various degree is exists. And at this present moment I feel some dormant pain at the back of my right lungs; I told the GP this and he dismissed it.

I am dying to see the people who diagnosed this at the Moorfields Eye Hospital, London, England, UK on 24th of February 2010, where they will confirm the 2nd ANCA blood test, which positive of PR3? or something.

At present I feel left in the dark; I have been prescribed 60mg Prednisalone and 20mg Omeprazole. I am now reducing the doses under instruction - they have set me to go down to 30mg, 25mg next week, 20g the following 15g the next then 10mg till the appointment.

WHAT DOES THIS MEAN?

The blur in the eye getting better, it is not better than what I had. I am experiencing a lot of burping and today it was the other way, flatulence.

As a result I got some;

Dandelion root - capsules for the digestive and kidney
Milk thistle - for liver
Liquorice for the lungs
Hawthorn for the heart

I have [not] taken any but looking for guidance if I should.

Thanks

Mayar Akash

Bruce replied back later in the day of Tuesday 2nd of February 2010

Received email: 5

(From: blades49456 <blades49456@sbcglobal.net, To: Mayar Akash <mayarakash@yahoo.com, Sent: Tue, February 2, 2010
11:30:28 PM, Subject: Re: [wgdiscussion] Re: Welcome to the group (was no subject))

Hello, Mayar.
I don't have enough knowledge to answer all your questions.

The burping and flatulence I can't comment on excepting to say
I've had some bouts of that, but it goes away. It could be
related to diet or meds or WG or ??

One does not deal with WG "through luck". One deals with it
medically, using a glucocorticoids at the start (Prednisalone or
similar) and an immunosuppressive such as azathioprine,
methotrexate, cyclophosphamide, etc. Any physician who
implies that "luck" plays a major role in treating WG probably
doesn't have much experience with WG, or similar
autoimmune vasculitides.

X-rays don't always show everything that WG could cause in
lungs. I had a 2 cm nodule that x-ray didn't detect, but CT scan
did. When you speak of a lesion, I assume you mean in your
lung. Please correct me if I'm wrong.

If your consultant isn't an expert in vasculitus, then his
dismissal of your symptoms may mean little. You need to be
seen by a vasculitus expert. I'm attaching a file with some
suggestions on physicians in the U.K., and on patient support
groups. Try to get a referral to one of those physicians, and
you may find one of the patient support groups helpful.

Prednisalone alone will rarely put WG into a quiet state
(remission). It usually takes some months of treatment with an
immunosuppressive, although unusually, Prednisalone and
Septra DS will be effective without an immunosuppressive.
Many rheumatologists in the U.S. put WG patient on Bactrim
DS (same as Septra DS) to prevent relapse of the WG. You
might ask about that at your next appointment. Rarely a light
case of WG may be treated with Prednisalone and Septra DS
only.

While on Prednisalone, cANCA and anti-PR3 test results will be more normal than they would be were you not on Prednisalone, and so would unlikely to correctly state the level of WG activity. I think most vasculitus experts judge the disease activity level more by symptoms than by blood test results. ANCA and anti-PR3 and anti-MPO don't always track WG activity.

Below 10 mg/day, the general consensus among WG patients seems to be to go in 1 mg increments, and take about 10-14 days at each level. Some even go slower. But the taper of prednisone from original 60 mg/day or whatever is usually only started after an immunosuppressive has suppressed the white blood cell (WBC) counts to somewhat below normal. The taper of Prednisalone sounds (by my opinion) a bit hasty. although getting you down to 10 mg so quickly may be deliberate to get a better idea of how active WG is.

If your GP or consultant isn't checking urine for creatinine level, they should be. WG can demolish kidneys in a weekend. Granted while you're on Prednisalone, WG isn't likely to damage kidneys, but it's responsible medicine to monitor kidney function in a WG patient with active WG. Later, you can monitor yourself using urine dipsticks. You can read something about that that I compiled at http://www.vasculitis-patient.com/7_medical_tests.php#Dipsticks

I think I first messaged you on Face book, but I have no record of that, and looking at the WG groups, I don't find you there. You might remind me of in which group you first posted.. There doesn't seem to be much of a place for herbal remedies in the treatment of WG. A non-inflammatory diet may help. See http://www.vasculitis-patient.com/14_nasal_dental_diet.php#Food   for some suggestions on what to eat and what to avoid.

I have NO medical training so nothing I say here or elsewhere should be taken to be medical advice. Refer all medical symptoms, problems, concerns, and questions to appropriate licensed medical professionals.

Best wishes for effective treatment of your WG and early improvement.

Bruce (WG '97) My web page on vasculitus: http://www.vasculitis-patient.com
(The slide out menus aren't working at this time, so navigation below major topics has to be done using the site plan).

Support the Vasculitus Foundation: http://www.vasculitisfoundation.org Join to receive their bimonthly newsletter.

Attend the Jul 30-Aug 1 Symposium in Long Beach CA See http://www.vasculitisfoundation.org/2010vasculitis-symposium

Don't forget that SAV patients can register with the Vasculitus Clinical Research Consortium at http://rarediseasesnetwork.epi.usf.edu/vcrc/index.htm

My return email on Wednesday 3rd of February 2010 to Bruce.

Sent email: 6

Hello Bruce,

Thank you for your reply.
I think it's from the medicine I'm taking, from Omeprazole
prescribed to me along with the Prednisalone. Late last year I
had the stomach bug helicobacter pylori infection which I was
treated with [an] antibiotic combination, I was told by the GP a
follow up stool test was not necessary. Having done research
then, Omeprazole reduces the acid and therefore the food
stay[s] in your guts longer, thus the burping and flatulence.

The GP gave me an explanation that the consultants at the
Moorfields eye hospital gave me Omeprazole with the
Prednisalone so that the Prednisalone doesn't burn a hole in my
stomach at that dose.

Yes the lesion was in my right lung. When the consultant told
[me] it was nothing, I [was] left with the question, how can it
be nothing, if the lesion is there and the x-ray & CT picked it
up.

I first joined the Wegener syndrome group and then Veronique
guided me to this group. I am on face book but not on any
groups, Mayar Akash.

The GP also said the same that "it must be serious for the
consultants to prescribe 60mg of Prednisalone".

The GP has not made any information available or follow-on
care plan. I think you are right, he doesn't have much
experience in this field.

I am looking at the following natural products:
Hawthorn berries - heart
Milk thistle   - liver
Dandelion roots   - kidney
Liquorice   - lungs
Grape seed extract - general
and as Cyndi highlighted - grape fruit seed
3.2.2010

Mayar Akash

Received email: 6

Hello, Mayar..

The problem with autoimmune vasculitus is that the T cells go a bit crazy and make antibodies that attack one's own tissues. So the problem is to damp down the immune system (and that has the undesirable side effect of making one more susceptible to opportunistic infection but that has to be tolerated). Most autoimmune vasculitides will kill the patient within a few years if not treated adequately.

Frankly, there's no scientific evidence of herbs, foods, food extracts etc. can actually adequately suppress the immune system enough. There's all sorts of claims on the internet, most trying to sell you something. Be very sceptical of claims that don't come from reputable medical sources.

An anti-inflammatory diet can help, or rather, pro-inflammatory foods should be minimized. The best "diet" I know of is the one in Dr. Barry Sears book, "The Zone" or his newer one (about the same really), "The Anti Inflammatory Zone". Five meals a day. A daily amount of protein based on one's activity level, spread approximately equally over the five meals. A calculated amount of carbohydrates with each meal, but ones with a low glycaemic index, which means fresh and lightly steamed vegetables, fresh fruits, very little bread, pasta, sugars, potatoes, etc. FYI, I followed that diet while on prednisone and didn't have the ferocious hunger that prednisone usually causes.

You can look at what Cyndi in CA put together on foods/herbs etc. as I reformatted it several years ago. She may have augmented her original list. I don't know.
See http://www.vasculitis-patient.com/Anti-Inflammatory_Foods.html or look at http://www.vasculitis-patient.com/14_nasal_dental_diet.php#Food

Regards, Bruce (WG '97)

My search continued and I came across information about groups in the United Kingdom and I emailed them following day of the 3rd of February.

From: blades49456 <blades49456@sbcglobal.net To: Mavar Akash <mavarakash@yahoo.com Sent: Wed, February 3, 2010 3:04:08 AM Subject: Re: [wgdiscussion] Re: liquorice

Sent email: 7

Hi

My name is Mayar Akash and I am a 37 year old Bangladeshi Male. I live in the East End of London. Over the Christmas period '09, I came down with a throbbing pain in the left eye and then I noticed blurring in my left eye. I got scared and went to my local A&E on the 26th of December. Being dissatisfied with [their] diagnosis of Conjunctivitis, I went to Moorfields eye hospital where they after the blood test ANCA came back positive of PR3, I was told I have WG. However, at this point it was not confirmed to me 100%. A second blood test has been taken and I await result on the 24th of this month.

I had been prescribed 60mg of Prednisalone with 20mg Omeprazole weeks before the blood test came back. Once I was given the indication what I had, I told the consultant that I will be researching this on the net, the consultant told me to hold back as I will not be able contextualise the information (but can anyone). As a result I came across the Wagner's syndrome group, who then pointed me to the WG group and there I found Cyndi & Bruce who have been very supportive. Bruce has given me this list with your details.

There are so many things that are opening up and its mind blowing as to what I am in now and what life is to become. This ratio of 20-30,000 - 1 is mind blowing. I am wondering how many people are affected in the UK. What services and support are there.

I am not confident with my GP's response; His projection of his knowledge & experience of this disease [has] left in the dark. His comments to me were "tough luck". During this time I was already informed of the prospect from my search and Veronique from the WS group directed me to the VS site. What is the state of play in the UK for WG & VS sufferers?

Thanking you in advance for your time and support.

Mayar Akash.

Received email: 7

Hi Mayar,

I'm sorry to hear you have joined what seems an ever-increasing number of people being diagnosed with vasculitus. I'm not sure that this means there are more people with the disease, just that the medical profession are getting better at recognising it!

I have had Wegener's Granulomatosis for the past 8 years (diagnosed when I was 42) and initially presented with an extremely red and sore eye (scleritis), amongst other symptoms. Large doses of steroids are often the first line of attack used by doctors when they suspect vasculitus to be the cause. Anyway, do wait until the doctors confirm your diagnosis since that can make a difference to both the on-going treatment and severity of your condition.

If you are keen to research the condition beforehand, do choose websites carefully as some are out of date and quite misleading. There is a good American website run by the Vasculitus Foundation (www.VasculitisFoundation.org) who also have leaflets on the various forms of vasculitus.

In the UK ARC (Arthritis Research) publish a leaflet on vasculitus which you should be able to pick up from your local hospital or, if you let me have your address I have a spare one I could send you, alternatively you could Google them and see if the leaflet is published on-line.

There is also a useful Yahoo group called Voice4Vasculitis which was set up in the UK by the husband of someone who has WG.

The group has members (fellow sufferers in the main so speaking from personal experience rather than any specialist medical knowledge) from around the world but a large number are from the UK and therefore comments and advice are particularly relevant to us here (VOICE4VASCULITIS@yahoogroups.co.uk).

Finally, there are local support groups which, many find very useful to join. I know that one is in the process of being set up close to Hammersmith Hospital (email Vincent Fernandes [vincentf51@hotmail.com] for details) although I'm not aware of one in the East End of London.

Do question your GP carefully – my experience is that GPs have very little knowledge of the condition and it is best to insist on being referred to a Consultant Specialist. If you are unhappy with the treatment you get at your local hospital you have the right to ask to be referred to hospitals which specialise in the condition – Hammersmith is one of them.

Finally, please bear in mind that WG and vasculitis in general is a strange condition that affects everyone differently – it is therefore very difficult to predict how it may affect you - and reading too much literature may scare you unnecessarily! We with WG often experience similar things but not necessarily all the same ones and not always at the same time – some people are diagnosed, treated and return to everyday life quickly whilst others may experience relapses and need more treatment.

My advice would be to keep positive but listen to your body when it tells you to rest etc as fighting it lengthens the recovery time – pacing yourself will make it much easier!

I do hope the hospital get your condition under control quickly and please do get back in touch if there are any questions you think I may be able to help answer.
Best wishes

Charlotte Stoner

stoners@talktalk.net" <the.stoners@talktalk.net, To: mayarakash@yahoo.com, Sent: Thu, February 4, 2010
Subject: Re: Seeking information, support, advise for WG)

Sent email: 8

<u>Sunday 7th of February 2010</u>

Hi Bruce,

I went through the food list. Cyndi has updated and has added Liquorices to the list. I have also started taking liquorice and Milk Thistle. I'll update if I notice any changes.

However, something's kicked in since the last email. My joints, especially my knees and hand aching burning in the morning, especially my right knee. The muscle between my thumb and index figure is sore and has cramp like pain.

My left arm (upper arm) muscle aches, carrying anything makes it ache; I started doing light stretches.

I've started a journal.
Thanks Mayar

Sent email: 9

Monday 8th of February 2010

Hi Charlotte,

I am beginning to get muscle aches in my arm on a regular basis. I have noticed that after I lift or carry items which I've wouldn't think twice to carry. I am 37 years of age, still young and fit. I know that pred. makes your muscle weak but I didn't think it would be so soon. I started taking Prednisalone in January 2010, my shoulders, biceps, forearm, my hands, all are aching. My left side started first and today I lifted a box about midday and now it's a nagging dull but nearer to the bone ache.

I have an appointment on the 24th of February 2010 with the consultants at the Moorfields Eye hospital, but I'm thinking if I can get over the counter Vitamin D3 or does it have to be prescribed. I am sceptical about my GP, if I go to them they will say I am being a hypochondriac.

I'm in a situation I have 3 people to ask. Yourself in the UK & Bruce and Cyndi in the forum. I look forward to your advice.

Mayar.

Received email: 8

Hi Mayar,

These aches and pains could be the vasculitus or the Prednisalone! It's very difficult sometimes to know whether the disease or the pills are causing symptoms. My advice would always be to consult with your doctor. If you do not have faith in your GP (you may want to think about changing the doctor you see?), why not phone the eye hospital and ask to speak to your consultant's secretary? I've done this in the past and found it the best way to get an answer quickly. Although the secretary will not have the answer he/she will pass the message on to the consultant who may ask to see you sooner or get someone to phone you about your concerns. I usually take this route as it cuts out the GP!

I don't know about taking vitamin supplements as I've always been wary about taking anything without checking with the consultant first - even over the counter medicines/supplements can interact badly with the strong medicines we are prescribed.

Hope this is helpful.
Best wishes, Charlotte

(From: "the.stoners@talktalk.net" <the.stoners@talktalk.net, To: mayarakash@yahoo.com, Sent: Mon, February 8, 2010 11:27:01 AM, Subject: Re: Seeking information, support, advise for WG)

I also got response from a group based in Oxford.

Received email: 9

"Mayar,

sorry to hear that you have joined the vasculitus club, but hopefully it sounds as if you may have been caught quite early and treated promptly.

I have had WG for 15 years this July and manage a normal life despite the drugs! I was 32 when diagnosed.

I run the Oxfordshire Vasculitus Support Group, I have attached some information about us, our latest newsletter and seminar info.

There are various local support groups around the UK (mainly in the south). Difficult to know the prevalence, we think that more people are being diagnosed, the knowledge by GP's etc now is better than 15 years ago. The main thing is to have a consultant who knows about vasculitus.

If you want to talk you can give me a call: 01295-816841
Our meetings are open to anyone who wants to come.

Vincent Fernandes has set up a London Support Group:

Hope has been helpful",
Sue Ashdown
OVSG

From: Oxfordshire vasculitis support group <oxonvsg@hotmail.com, To: mayarakash@yahoo.com, Sent: Wed, February 10, 2010 6:08:39 PM

Subject: RE: Seeking information, support, advise for WG

Sent email: 10

<u>Thursday 11th of February 2010</u>

Hi Sue,

Thank you for your email and the information very much appreciated as I feel very alone with this where I am.

I will be reading the attachments and making contact as soon as I am able.
Mayar

NB: *Please note that the information in the email section was written in 2010 and will be out of date. Please check all links and information for updates on-line. The knowledge about Wegener's Granulomatosis is always being discovered.

While I was emailing the groups about my condition, it was clear that it was visible to my older brother and his family. I also took note and re-assessed my situation and self.

I was not in my own stable home, I did not have anyone who would be able to take care of me, I would be burdening my brother's family, this I understand, nor can they comfort or console me. My brother spoke to me about going back to Bangladesh, where mum and dad were. There, I would get the love, attention and care that I would require.

I did not refuse as I knew I didn't want to become a "lab rat" but I knew I had an appointment with a Moorfields Eye Hospital consultant, where I would learn more definitive knowledge about my disease. The flight was planned and arranged days after the hospital appointment.

Setting off

Culmination of everything had come to this one point in life, all of my years and all of me and about me, as days became hours and hours became minutes, to boarding the plane to go to Bangladesh.

Packing the luggage yet unpacking the mind, the dreams, aspirations, the attachments, sentimental, paternal, emotional, mental and residual, they had become hoarded baggage that was of no use to me for where I was going and the purpose.

I felt that I was boarding a plane to my death; I was going there to die – to live through the effects of the disease and make peace with myself and pass over. I did not want any looking back on the children, or the 'exs' and wife, sterilising my heart and my feelings. I didn't want to feel and deal with useless emotional attachments, only to handle the pain that the disease was throwing at me - I could cope with both. It was easier said then done, as I found it hard to come to terms with some aspects more than others; some I was done with and they did not affect me, especially all the unnecessary dramas.

Severing of the bonds with my children proved hard, both mentally and emotionally. However, residually and physiologically I could not detach - they were part of my soul. I knew I was taking them with me, my son Samir and my daughter Amaani. They were my trophies in this mortal earthly life as a human - I was going to return to the astral plains with two stripes on my uniform.

While the clock was ticking, I could feel so many things happening, such as thoughts, memories, issues, vengeance, hurt, pain just shredding off me. Falling, off-loading, dumping, bleeding of the senses - a steady stream of activity was pouring out of me and I could feel it like a trail or a tail coming out of me as I walked, sat and slept.

I was not going take that weight to the airport and board the plane with them. I left much of my spent life here in UK before boarding the plane, so that I could be focussed and clear about the predicament that I had and would need to deliver myself through. All that I knew I had to focus on was how I was going to manage the pain, the pain from my small veins solidifying in my organs; I had already had a 'taster' with my eyes.

How would I deal with the pain from a stroke, or a heart attack, or the second eye etcetera, etcetera. My dad had suffered a stroke and that I had witnessed. I lived through his stroke with him but had not felt the distress within him. I would have to deal with the same if I survived the attack. Oh … the unknown, the fear, the anxiety of the unknown; inside my 'innards' were adopting, re-opting, assessing, re-evaluating, recalculating - preparing for the immediate, short and long term - an introspective person in analysis.

Boarding the car, checking in, catching a cup of tea with my siblings before going into the departure lounge; the hugs and the good byes; farewells, all in a bubble, in a protective mode, so many shut-offs, so much numbness, I saw everything and caught every thing but everything was muffled and mute as I detached myself from the hugs. I was not going to share my misfortune with them. I was leaving, walking down the path to the departure lounge to die; there was not going to be any further emotional or mental baggage to take with me.

I was physically there on the plane but emotionally numb and mentally mute and as the plane lifted off the tarmac and we became disconnected from England, I was deep in introspections until we landed and I disembarked from the plane. I passed over, I was leaner and lighter and focussed on the next stages of my life. My mind was open and had to adjust to all that would now unfold.

When the pilot announced that we were approaching the Dhaka Airport to land, my head and mind changed to anticipation, not knowing what to expect and looking out of the window I was able to catch sight of the building tops as well as the emerald green rice fields and the hills.

https://www.youtube.com/watch?reload=9&v=eqT8AK_6-DU

This is a typical view, this image taken from an internet source to assist the mind.

From Dhaka airport, I caught the transit flight to Sylhet to Osmani International Airport, where I was going to be collected by someone sent by my parents.

It kept running through my mind - I had gone to Bangladesh one way, knowing that I was going there to die and I would not be returning back.

https://iccia.com/?q=islamicTourism/airports&ctr=Bangladesh

Travelling to Bangladesh meant a change of weather and climate. It was hot and humid for most months of the year and the sun was out... sunshine. It was a dramatic change from London, where it was grey, cloudy, dull, cold and rainy. Most of the time, its gloom had added to all other predicaments that were inherent with the place.

In Bangladesh the heat from the sun immediately uplifted me. My mood was upbeat. I felt light, my body was warm to hot, sweating and perspiring. The heat and humidity changed my mind-set. I was thirstier so had to keep myself hydrated.

This was a sight for sore eyes.

This is the gate into my father's house, with newly-laid soil to raise the ground up to the street level. The coconut tree in front of the red, pink and white building just eased the sight and mind.

Generally, the mood of the community and surrounding is positive, light-hearted and upbeat. The hustle and bustle of the towns and market spaces and then the calm, tranquil and sereneness of the village and countryside.

The dramatic change in the temperature from the UK to Bangladesh meant that for me I was hot nearly all of the time, day and night, even in the shade or by a fan. The only time one could be cool to cold was in a room with air conditioning or having a cold shower or dip in the ponds. I did not 'do' ponds due to my being a weak swimmer and the water being full of natural, possibly unpleasant elements. I kept myself in the shade and I wore light clothing; my dress sense changing to deal with the hot climate.

Even though I was there with my illness, there were others who were less fortunate than me, who were the poor who were old and frail, ill or unable to work and those who were alone with no children or partner to look after them.

The forecourt was bare and empty when I got there.

There was a pond with bamboos supporting its banks so that it did not cave in.

My Parents

Mum collected me at Sylhet airport and we drove down to our villa which is 35km southwest of Sylhet town. It was very emotional time for me as I was feeling so fragile, fragile from the knowledge of my illness and from the effects of the steroids I was taking.

I was sobbing, my mum was sobbing and my dad, too, was crying. My parents had been told by my older brother about what was happening to me. I cannot recall back exactly but I was like a crying baby, bursting into tears every time I spoke for a couple of weeks and then I recall settling down.

I was witnessing my mum and dad crying with me and for me. I knew they had already lost a child before me and now finding out that I could die before them could not have been easy for them to comprehend.

My dad was so gentle and caring towards me, watching over me, while he himself was being looked after by mum. The house was emotional and I recall feeling sombre in the beginning. I remember mum being mum - she was singing and was making light of things with the worker they had in the house.

My mum tending to the garden.

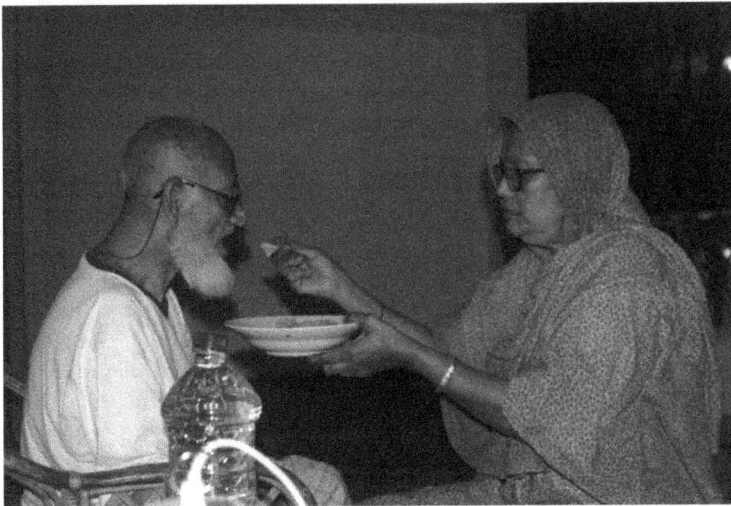

So many beautiful things were happening to me being around my mum and dad - the innocence of the paternal, maternal and child dynamics in a non-challenging and non-demanding setting. It was my father's house, he who was the owner of the land - it was a great backbone of a feeling.

Lamenting

I found myself searching, soul-searching, searching my mind.
I sorted and re-sorted, dismantling myself.

I hit highs and lows.

My misspent youth lead – I was sobbing

I found myself alone, lonely, isolated within a personal darkness. The spiritual growth had taken over but the personal worthiness and value was hanging low within.

I was going to die and had my life been of worth? Had it been of any value to others? What was my benchmark, was it measured with love and if so, by who in particular? All love and specifically, "was I ever loved", did another soul love me, warts and all?

This period of my life was turbulent, as if I was on high, stormy seas with the clashes and smacking of the waves, water and wind.

I felt rotten, a waste of space and that I had not made an impact in anyone's life.

If I was going to die, I wanted to know that I had added value to world, that my live had been purposeful, that I had made some functional input for humanity and humankind.

I was low - low in morale, spirit, energy, faith, failure, failure as a human soul. I was in pain but not one that could be alleviated with pain killers. It was the pain of a rotting, rotting soul. I was rotten, a waste of a human, a waste of a human soul, one that could surely not appeal to any other soul.

What kind of the person was I?

Was I not appealing to anyone?

Could not anyone recognise me?
Could anyone like me for who I was?

All I could see was how people used me and how I did not allow people to come close to me because of that reason.

This process also highlighted some, if not, many of my ailments; fear of intimacy, my mindset, attitude, my own projections of me.

Oh I was sobbing, crying, lamenting out, I was lost, I was cold, I was in the dark, there was no time, there was no time of return.

My every limb was crying, aching with the knowledge of "I will be no more".

Alone, no children around, no partners, no siblings nor friends. NO moral support, no support.

It was about my autonomy, it's what I did, it was about what I have to show, what I ... it was about me, me, me.

I found myself isolated in a desert with the horizon on all sides.

In my lamentation I was so desolate and destitute to learn if someone other than my own blood loved me for who I was. I sent out that "s.o.s" out to the universe. I did not know then but I was projecting my pain out to the universe.

Gardening

A couple of days after settling in , I noticed there was a tree stump, in the side of the building, so I took the opportunity to whack at it. I took a localised axe and I was pounding it. I knew what I was doing and wanting to get my rage, anger, hurt, pain, disappointment, loathing frustration, hate, betrayal, self pity, aggression out, out with every strike. I held the handle with both my hands and raised above and over my head, and as I did that I focussed on my emotion, clear in my mind and thought; and I let go of all by energy in bringing it back over my head, in full stretch upon the stump, whack, thud, pound, it landed, made contact; it just dug, cut in to the wood; release!

I felt that quench, quench of the weight, blockage in my heart, my thoughts, inhibitions, felt my mind lightening up. I exerted myself in each blow, each strike; each time I was attacking my woes and mental foes. I pounded until I was completely knocked up out in a very hot and humid day; the sun was beating down on me and all the while I was sweating profusely. It felt good, I felt good, I knew that I had been thinking of doing this back in the UK but had not known I was going to be doing it in Bangladesh. It was one of many of my attempts to help myself and this went on to become the beginning of further hands-on gardening.

The villa had an acre of land in front of the house and being a keen gardener, I started paying attention to gardening. I started by landscaping the front. I was digging, shovelling earth and straightening the path to the main gate to the outside world. I started getting flowers from the local nurseries and from neighbours and planting them in the yard and also in pots. The earth was so fertile that everything grew. This was such a good feeling and when the saplings rooted and then started shooting leaves and flowers that, too, was a wonderful feeling.

I turned to planting terracotta pots and then wanted to surround the front of the building with them.

I bought rose plants, various local flowers, fruit trees and shrubs and I planted them all around the villa. I also purchased a large quantity of hedgerow saplings and planted them along the pathway, to and from the house. I kept myself busy - I committed my time to nature, physically investing in God, God's outdoors, the earth, the soil that we all will be buried in.

Through gardening I was getting close to the earth; touching it, feeling it and contacting it to my skin; becoming one with it. I was bonding with it, emotionally, mentally and physically; the smell of it, the feeling of the texture with my hands and feet, when it was dry, wet, damp and sun-scorched dry. It was my way of getting to know the earth that I was going to be resting in.

I was also fulfilling another aspect of me, my appreciation of beauty in God's creations of flower and fauna. I was planting all sorts of flower from red ones to white, pink, yellow, peach, violet to purple, magenta and the various shades of green. The colours were awesome and I was in colour therapy.

Creating Amaani Garden

All of the rose plants in the terracotta pots then got re-planted in the plot in front of the house. During this time, I mentally created a symmetrical design in mind and I started arranging the rose plants. In my heart, I was thinking of my daughter while I was planting, so it became the Amaani garden. Within the Amaani garden I then had thoughts about the other women in my family who I missed - my sister Sheila, my dadi Romzan Banu both of whom I never saw, then there was my nani Momtaz, who I saw and she had dedicated twenty seven years of her life living and looking after my

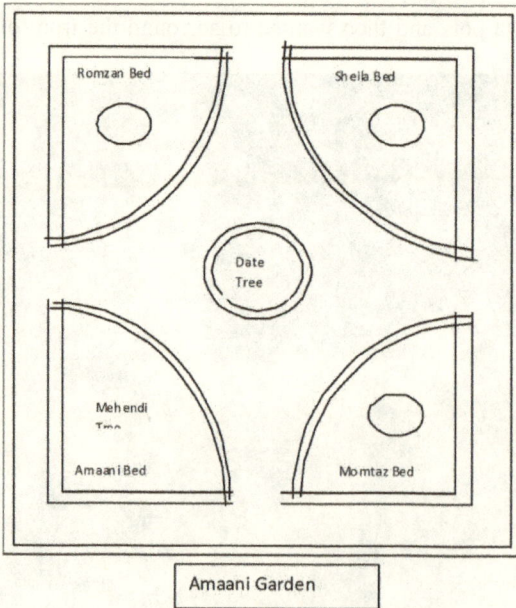

Amaani Garden

father's place, where she died. So I named the four beds within the garden after them and planted a tree in each of them. The Amaani bed had a mehendi tree; she liked mehendi.

Bang in the middle I planted a date tree. I had this vision of the tropics with the palm leaves spread out like an umbrella; whoever sits there can catch the shade.

The garden is still in need of the further work to get it to the complete vision. How I imagined it. White walkways as well as the raised brick walls that mark out the garden with lights.

Disclosure
It was another beautiful day, on the rooftop of my father's building under the shadows of the Maringa tree. I was always taking photographs from the roof top while enjoying the hot breeze in the shade. My mother came up to the roof to touch base with me and it is then I got a voice in my head - to tell her my withheld information about me, her son. I got an opportunity and took it because I was in the mindset that I was going to die, so there was nothing to lose, told her that I been abused …by one of her relatives.

That this was the reason why I got so agitated when she mentioned his name or talked about him. She said why had I not told her this before, it is not that easy, I just could not. I am not sure how she felt inside but I felt I just off-loaded an airport with jumbos.

This had been inside me for decades along with other similar ills. They had festered and boiled in me to the point where they had outwardly affected my personality, behaviour and mannerisms. I was no longer trusting of people; I didn't make friends easily and preferred my own company. Some people found me cold and recluse.

This was a release, relief and a closure on one hand and then the knowledge that I had exposed my fragile part of my life on the other but I wasn't going to dwell on it, as it was done and it needed to be done, as clear cut as that - that was how I was processing myself then.

I also recall my thought processes to adapt, in my mind I knew I had made a one way trip to live the rest of my days and die in this country. So, therefore, I had to become more like the people, get accustomed to the way of living, their attitude and mannerisms. I made myself think of my takas than the pounds because normally I would not think twice about spending pounds but there, things are much cheaper than what they are in the UK and also we would be visiting for only a short time.

Not to be overly generous with the dispensing of the money, not to overpay or knowing get shafted as this was how the system was set up in Bangladesh. Traders and locals can smell a foreigner or tourist miles away and as a result hike up their prices, by as much as 400-500%, so I started watching the takas, haggling prices and choosing carefully where I was going to buy from.

I had to be aware of the current affairs of the area and the hierarchical system. It is definitely who you know over there what matters and determines your safety. So, knowing people of the political network are of benefit, as you or your family would not be openly targeted - fraudsters.

Being from the UK and having grown up in East London, talking was not my strong point and, in particular, the long-winded conversation, which is how most of the conversation took place back home. I would be like 'get to the point' and they would feel disrespected; I was told that there was no sweetness in my conversation. Yes, this was nothing new to me but to be told so in Bangladesh, I did have a self reflection on it and knew that if I was going to live out here I will have to make some adjustments to fit in.

In order to fit in, I realised that there was not much to change as a way of going backwards because, what I observed, other than bathing, everything thing else was available in the town for a fee, from laundry to shaving, hair cutting, ironing, eateries, confectionaries, nail cutting, earwax cleaning, massaging and so on.

This was an eye opener; I had so many hang-ups, shaving, ironing etc, no biggy over there, just get them done; cost-wise they were British pennies. Every morning I would have freshly-ironed clothes, go and have a shave and then stroll back and have something to eat at home or have something in the bazaar.

The attitude of life and living was going notches down the gears - chill out, take life and living in a stride; it is how the system works there in Bangladesh; the system supports a very large economical structure cascading down.

Wow, this was changing and shaping my attitudes and expectations, it felt good being able to hang up my hang-ups; discharging the pent-up energy; chipping away Britishness. British Bangladeshis only know just how British they are until they go back to Bangladesh. In the UK, we are diluted and accustomed to the localities we live and grow up in. Our community is more conservative, preserving the traditions and customs but in Bangladesh we are more open as there is no other ethnic community, other than our Hindu neighbours. Even then, much of our customs are similar.

There, my mind had to re-adjust to accommodate whatever arose on the day. A person begging was one of them and it was always the same people asking. Months in, I was developing my own strategies in how to manage them and the dispensing of my money.

I formulated the following system that if I knew I was going to visit a place more than once then I would not pay anything to anyone until the last day. That way I managed the day, my money and people's attitude and expectation. The beggars have photographic memories and remember you, so if you give to them on the first day then you are sucked in thereafter and if you do not pay on the first day, then they are wary, wondering whether you will payout or not and so do not exhaust you.

It is not that I am tight but, situations at the tourist hotspots can become very abusive and animated. The small ones will not leave you alone and will have run miles down the slow street behind the vehicle. I also asked adult beggars whether it mattered to them where the money came from; I was received with a blank face, so I put it to them that if this was my only money that I had acquired from selling one of my kidneys, would that make any iota of a difference to them - no comment, blank face.

This re-education was making changes in me that I was not able to gauge straight away. I also learnt lessons by not giving alms to those who genuinely needed but fell into my category.

I had more than one incident where a beggar had come to me and I had declined or given just a little, then hours later I was stopped by a traffic cop and made to fork out hundreds of Taka. So there were many social lessons being taught to me about life and living.

When I realised what was happening to me, that I was there for a spiritual journey of my life, I regretted not giving anything to a handful of beggars and was very sorry to the point where I raised my hands, cried and prayed and in my prayers I gave away any good deeds that I may have earned through my life time to them. So after this point, I had no good deeds to call my own.

These were humbling moments still, being brought down, checking reality and being told to re-evaluate through divine interventions. To become totally compassionate and not selective was one; to freely give irrespective of the amount. It was not the fact I did not give - it was the mindset criteria that I developed to be "black or white", give or not give and being harsh and uncompassionate in executing it.

In the end, I gave the old, dearest possession that I had - whatever good deeds and blessing that I may have had, whether one or a million, it did not matter. I gave them all to those handfuls of people who came to me. I was rested in my mind that I may die with none; that was the deal of my life.

Prior to those moments, I had lost sight and those interventions made me believe that money was not everything in life; people's blessings were the golden nuggets we take with us and that gave me courage and strength to know that I was not dying empty, those deeds would go with me.

One mid-day, during lunch time, we were eating when we heard a loud banging noise at the front gate, off the road. It was a vagabond who had travelled from a shrine in Sylhet over thirty kilometres away and he wanted money. So, I told him that he would not get any money but he could certainly have a meal. He was given food and he ate outside while we finished our meal.

Once I had finished, we met him in the forecourt where he started speaking about my mother's fall and how she had hurt herself. Mum and I looked at each other, because only the day before, she slipped on the wet grass and hurt herself. We were both shocked and astonished. He was still asking for money.

He then randomly asked me the following question "If people do wrong, is God responsible?" It may have been an inadvertent question from him.

But then, this question began to take everything to another level, him being there. I did not understand the question at first but a few seconds later, as the question sunk in, something awoke in my dormant mind.

Now... I was abused as a young child. Afterwards, when I understood what had happened to me, I began to question God. "Why didn't he stop the people doing those fiendish acts?" There was no answer and ever since then I had held God responsible and felt that God had lost me and I held him in contempt. As that phase of my life happened I then found my salvation in the song, "Greatest Love of All", sung by Witney Houston. This song gave me the grounding that I needed and I questioned everything; about God, about religion and about people. One of the most profound things I learned was that God, physically, does not stop anyone! People stop themselves; people who are God-loving and also God-fearing; in worshipping God through love and fear, through their reverence in God they stop themselves from doing fiendish acts; (subjective) but generally amongst the pious people, it seems. God had no physical capacity to intervene. So God had no reverence to me. I charged God for letting it happen and not protecting me.

So in those few moments his question reverberated in me and the above just gushed into my head and I had the compulsion to answer his question with "NO".

Immediately, in that instant, a world of weight was lifted from my mind as if disappearing in a puff of smoke. I looked at the guy, went over to him, stretched my arm and offered him my open hand to shake his hand in doing so, I embraced him and gave him a hug.

In experiencing that and realising what had happened, he received few takas, which was what he wanted in the first place, he didn't do badly, as he got the money and also had a full meal. This was a profound encounter which left its mark on me and also my healing process. He had come from the monkey shrine in Sylhet town and he had somehow bled the bad blood I had towards God. He facilitated the cleansing and re-addressing the chemical imbalance that made my immune system turn on me.

Another occasion where I was blessed was when I visited my family's shrine. It is near my father's original village and was where I was born. Near there lies our ancestral shrine of Shah Mullah Mubarak Shahab, a Sufi saint. I went to visit and pay my respects. It was a very dry, bright day and the sun was out.

The shrine was clean and dry with a canopy over it to provide shade and also a breeze. I went in and I started to recite prayers and then went into contemplation. I was having a conversation with the saint as well as my grandfather and the all the other ancestors who were buried there.

After a while I felt like lying down on the right hand side of the tomb, so I laid flat next to the grave of the Sufi saint. I cannot remember exactly for how long I did this but it was at least a few minutes and as I closed my eyes, I felt relaxed as the setting was serene and tranquil. I felt calm and at peace with myself with no inhibitions at all. There was no one there; I was on my own, my chaperone was waiting in the vehicle a good distance away.

Sent email: 11

<u>Saturday 27th March 2010</u>

Hi Bruce,

24th Feb came and I went to get the 2nd blood test result for ANCA. The Dr didn't give me a definite answer but informed me that they will ask the GP to refer me to see a immunologist. They also got me to get another blood test "cat Scratch".

I was very unhappy with the fact that they did not explain anything to me.

Since then I've flown out to Bangladesh to my parents. I am continuing to take the Prednisalone and Omeprazole. After [a] couple of weeks I felt tingling and then pins and needles in my right arm. Upon investigating I noticed 2 lumps on the vein of the inside of my elbow. As a response I increased the Prednisalone from 10mg to 20mg. The pins and needles have reduced but the lumps are still there.

I am planning to get a full body MRI and try to locate someone who is aware of Vasculitus in Bangladesh. So far there is no known specialist.

Love to hear from you.

Mayar Akash

Received email: 10

Hello, Mayar.

I'm sorry you've returned to Bangladesh, though I can understand you felt you needed to do that. There are experts in England, and in London who could perhaps have been better than anyone you'll find in Bangladesh (but naturally, I can't know that).

The GP in London should have done a bit of homework to find you an appropriate rheumatologist when you were diagnosed. I assume the GP didn't explain very much to you because he/she wasn't knowledgeable enough to be able to explain.

As you've been diagnosed with WG, then the treatment should be that which has proven effective over time, high dosage prednisone (Prednisalone) on the order of 50-60 mg/day or higher, and an immunosuppressive such as Cellcept, methotrexate, Imuran, etc., or even cyclophosphamide if that's what it takes. I'm disturbed that you're looking for dietary solutions to a serious immune system malfunction. WG can do severe damage in a matter of a couple of days if it's aggressive.

The lumps in veins in your elbow are not a good sign. It's obvious that your disease is not adequately controlled.

I sincerely hope you can find a physician where you are that knows autoimmune vasculitides such as Wegener's Granulomatosis. If you don't find one soon and get effective treatment, it might be well to travel to where you can find the necessary expertise.

There's plenty of sound medical information on the internet. There's every reason to think your physician in Bangladesh can find what he/she needs in terms of treatment methods and options. If your physician doesn't do that, please find one who will. You have to be a persistent advocate for yourself, and if you don't feel up to it, have a family member or friend accompany you to appointments to ask questions and write down answers.

Please be aggressive about finding effective treatment. WG is too dangerous to be let go.

Regards, Bruce (WG '97)

(From: blades49456 <blades49456@sbcglobal.net, To: Mayar Akash <mayarakash@yahoo.com, Sent: Sat, March 27, 2010 7:16:47 PM, Subject: Re: lumps in my vein)

Sent email:12

<u>Thursday 1st of April 2010</u>

Thank you Bruce.

Just to assure you I am not looking for a dietary solution but I have always been a healthy-eating conscious person. You have been the only person who advised me on this subject and I've looked to you for support and guidance. The guidance you have given me, I value and respect. I will see what I can get with the local GPs.

I am pursuing leads for a immunologist in Dhaka the capital of Bangladesh. At present I am taking 20mg of Prednisalone, I will increase the dose to 30mg as the lump hasn't decreased but the pins and needles/tingling has reduced to unnoticeable. A faint blur in the left eye still exists.

I will ask a local GP to look into prescribing me an immunosuppressive.

Await your advice.

Mayar Akash.

The Medical Journey

Self-medicating

One of many things I learnt on this journey is that what is restrictive and expensive here in the West, UK and America, is readily available over-the-counter in Bangladesh.

Sample image of a pharmacy where I purchased some of my medicine while in the capital city Dhaka.

All the world's medicine, whether new, old or banned, are in use and available for cash.

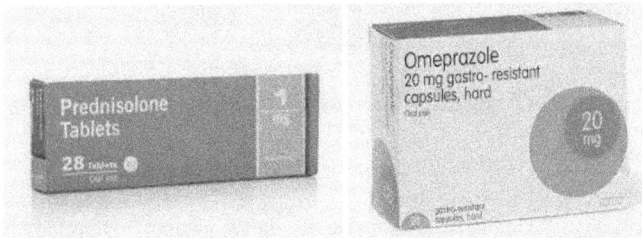

Sample images from the web.

So during my stay in Bangladesh, I was self-medicating with Prednisalone (steroids). I understood the process and the reasoning behind the steroid taking and the tapering down and up of it. To go in high to attack the disease and pain and then bring it back down, based on the diseases activity inside you increase and decrease the dose.

So, that is how I managed my medication while I was there, (I am not advocating this but I found myself in a region that had no idea about my disease.) The professionals in the UK were furious with me for doing that, as I could have been putting myself at further risk.

One of the consequences of taking Prednisalone is the reduction in vitamin D3 and the effect of its deficiency. The blood test showed that I was down to 40% and I had to build that back up. I am told that I was fortunate about the vitamin D3, as for some people, it is not easy to top it up again.

I went to the government-owned hospital in Dhaka, seeking a Rheumatologist who would advise me on what to do.

Difficulties

The underlying issues are many in Bangladesh and one of them that affected me in many ways was a regional one. The Dhaka professionals do not accept diagnoses of professionals in the town I was from, Sylhet.

The practices in Sylhet are looked down upon by the Dhaka professionals - that is so for all regions of the country. There is long history of issues between the Sylheti and Dhaka. Sylhet's wealth comes from money injected in from the UK and other western countries where Sylhetis reside.

Another aspect, simply staring me in the face was that you pay for your services so to take the opinions of others would mean that they lose out. So, I had to spent money in both parts. However, the diagnosis in Dhaka was superior to Sylhet's and over-rode the Sylheti Diagnosis.

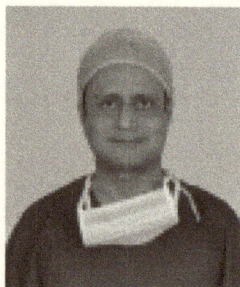

Dr Minhaj Rahman Chowdhury, MMBS, FCPS, MD, DTCD, FACR (USA)
Rheumatologist - Bangabandu Sheik Mujib Medical University.
Consultation/Operates from Japan Bangladesh Friendship Hospital
Address: 55 Satmasjid Road, Zigatola Bus Stand) Dhaka - 1209 Bangladesh
Phone+880-2-9672277

My local doctor and GP sign-posted me to another hospital - we travelled to locate him and made an appointment. He was not available but we found out that there were more doctors with the same expertise in Bangladesh. Dr Minhaj was not the first choice.

Dr Minhaj also works for the government hospital in Dhaka, the Sheikh Mujib Bangabandu Hospital. We had to make couple of visits to get an appointment as it is not as straightforward as in the west in terms of

- the waiting around
-then trying to get a place in the hospital to stay,
-the haggling,
-the going through various checks and tests
-it was good to have a local guide with me as he just about got me jumping through the queues … money talks.

Japan Bangladesh Friendship Hospital

Birdem Hospital
Then the Birdem Hospital, where they did the C ANCA tests the results came back negative - but I was on Prednisalone and that put doubts on the results.

It was like I was in a supermarket for medical tests - I had the scans, tests, from blood to urine, to chest x-ray, to the eye and then MRI of my brain.

It required travelling around - getting to know the area as well -

"Out of the frying pan into the fire!"

An ANCA test was done on the 12.5.2010 and the result came back seven days later. It came back negative but that did not make things better or conclusive.

I was in Bangladesh where it is hard to put one's trust in the medical profession. After all the consultation and tests, the next step was to start on the next level of medicine. I just had to live with the fact that I had WG and had to take steroids which were helping to ease the disease and it was in control. But, I was none the wiser and the doctor did not have any real experience in the disease and he wanted to put me on **Cytoxan** (see Cyclophosphamide).

What was promising was that Birdem had a department which specialised with Lupus and other autoimmune disorders, where I suppose it would have been a better place to start from. All the hospitals have their own website, so everyone can check out for the latest information, check out their Face book page.

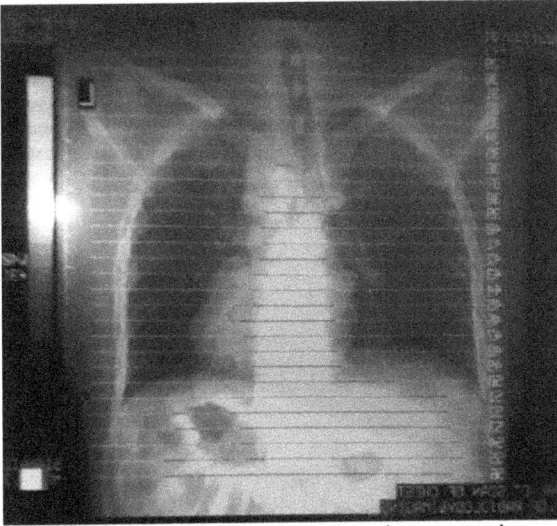

OMG! - Fright or flight moment! I had left the UK because I had not wanted to be an experimental guinea pig but here I was being given a medicine that would cause cancer.

Wow! No! OMG! This was out of the frying pan and into the fire. I could feel and see the difference the steroids were having and could see from the test results what was going on inside. The way I was feeling was not comfortable but to start taking a pill that was going to give me cancer for definite, I could not knowingly do that to myself.

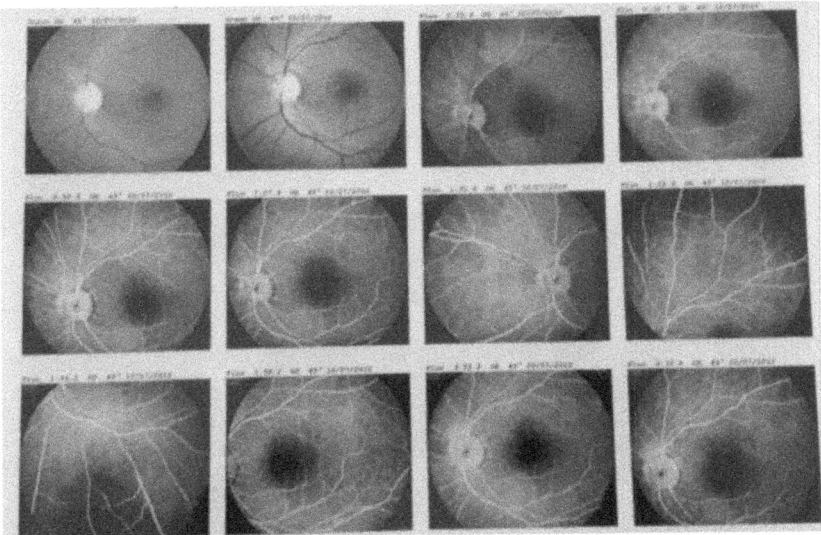

The test was done on the 10th of July 2010, [as I rewrite the 7th draft on 9.7.2020, tomorrow it will be 10 years]

Fortunately, Bruce had given me much information and also Bruce was there for me. (see emails)

> *"The Dr could not determine the next course of action from the result of the tests. Personally I will need to get second opinion as the medical profession in Bangladesh is full of "floors", however the rheumatologist is reputable as he is recognised as one of the 3 specialist in the country.*
>
> *His is with the view that until I am tapered off Prednisalone then I need to do a retest and see what is the situation with me. I have already started tapering myself and am experiencing various discomforts, from joint clicking and popping, discomfort under my lower rib cage and mental block - to standing idle having forgotten; I'm having to think for long moments (pauses). The Dr wants to put me on Cyclophosphamide - I have Googled this and I am not happy with the effects of this. I am seeking your guidance and advice on this medicine- to me it's a suicide pill. Under the situation and condition I am in, is it necessary to take this medicine - is this the only medicine that I can take or is there others -such as Imuran and or others. Since I left the hospital - this has been on my mind - a pill that will guarantee me cancer.*
>
> *It's quite possible that I don't know what is really happening with me. It is also clear that I don't have an overview of my life with*

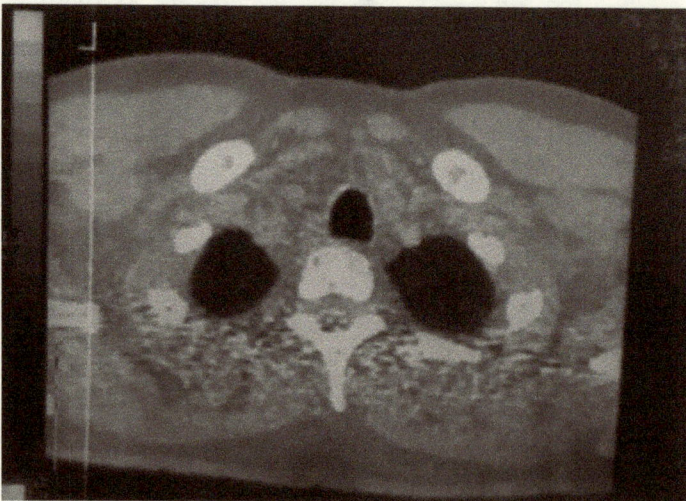

*Wegener's and in the long run. How long can I hold off before I
need to take the - Cyclophosphamide - or the alternatives - at what
stage?"*

This was hard, like somebody had trodden on my fingers - wow, there was so
much going through my head; it was as if I was being given a gun to shoot
myself, like Russian roulette with all the bullets in the barrel.

It was the thought of the pain and the suffering, the treatments, procedures
and the unknown that engulfed me. All the images of chemotherapies that I
had seen over the years flooded in my mind. The image of the dialysis, the
long sessions, the hair loss and life alteration, people, the obligation of a carer
and so on.

- Who was I going to turn to?
- Who was going to be there with me?

I am a loner, I will do it alone that was the resolve in me which stopped me
from breaking down, falling apart; naturally my instincts kicked in - my
survival mode.

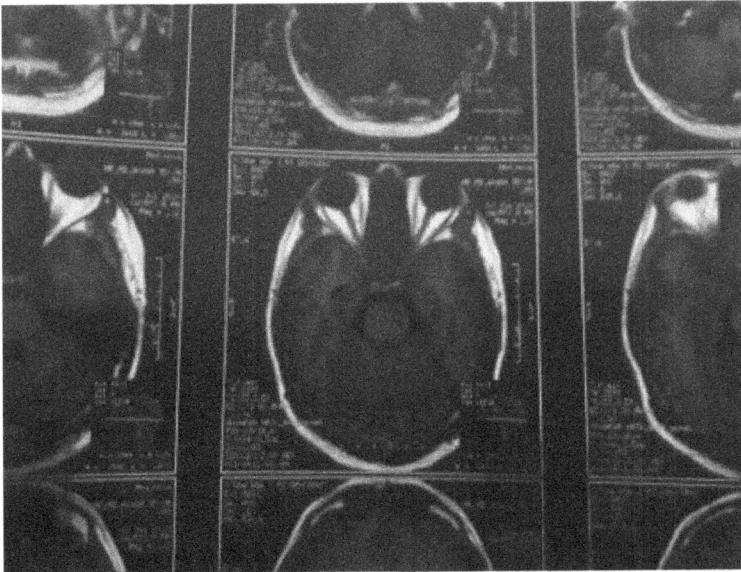

Accommodation

My experience of spending time in the hospital was an eye-opening one; it was nothing like my experience in England. When you go in for surgery in the UK you automatically are allocated a bed. Patients and their family have to arrange the accommodation beforehand.

It is probably not the same in all the other private hospitals; many of them are foreign and have various levels of service. However, because of the nature of my illness and treatment, I had no choice but to go to the government-run hospital as the consultants also worked and operated there. These professionals were some of the elite in their field in Bangladesh.

I had to go to the counter of the hospital for almost a week just to book a bed in one of the dormitories. This was a new experience and queuing up every day was challenging - usually money gets you the things you want and need but here it was proving to be difficult.

These experiences also ensured that I was equal to everyone that was queuing up for a bed - without it I was not going to get the treatment and investigation. I sat with people from all over the country and especially those that could not afford the private ones, but reflecting back it was more to do with the type of treatment required.

Every morning I went to the allocations desk in the foyer on the ground floor, until I got a slot at the hospital. I had to stay in a hotel a few miles away and travel to the hospital by a particular time. The weather was hot and made the travelling bearable - the opposite would be cold and raining as in England; this doom and gloom would have made it all the more expressing. For me, the novelty of the city was still new and it would take a while before it wore off, the travelling up and down with the CNG - the three wheeler motor car - was a novelty, but this was something that did not last long, because of the noise and vibration.

http://theamericanswillcome.blogspot.com/2013/03/the-auto-rickshaws-cng.html

CNG (Compressed Natural Gas)

Compressed Natural Gas lives up to its name, respecting its gaseous form and kept at room temperature, while subject to major pressure (about 200 bars). Its very nature makes it the alternative to everyday fuel in cities, thanks to how it meets the energy needs of light vehicles, such as vans, buses, rubbish trucks, etc. In other words, it caters for urban or mid-distance journeys, while also being suitable for short freight routes of between 300 and 500 kilometres. It is also compatible with renewable gas, making its CO_2 footprint virtually non-existent.

The accommodation in the hospital was reasonable, in no way of any stars as it was simply a white-tiled cubicle with toilet and shower facility. The bed was of metal frame and a mattress.

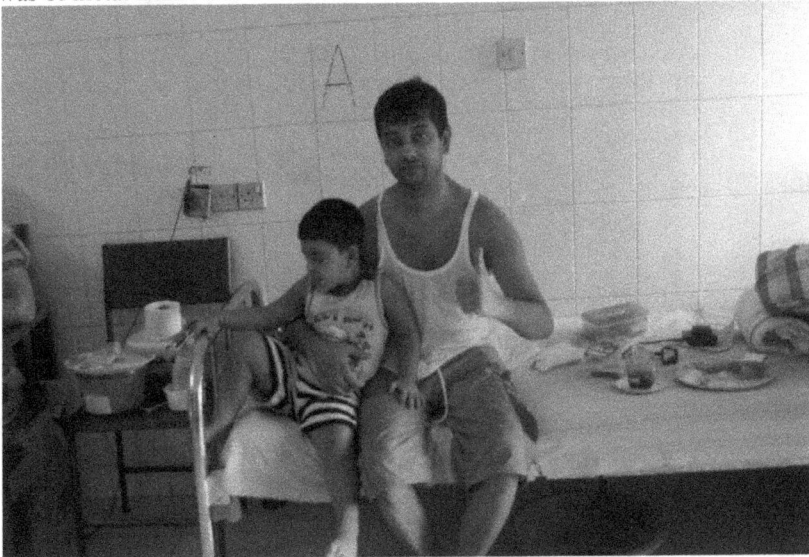

As you can see in the photograph, the beds are marked with a letter, made using a marker pen on the tiled wall. The electrics were basic but they did the job.

I shared it with another patient, brother Monir and his family, his wife, his two daughters and his son-in-law, who spent a lot of time in there, they also looked after me too. They ended up providing home-cooked meals - lunch and dinner. We all sat down together and ate and the food was delicious. Ten years on and I can still taste some of the dishes in the back of my throat!

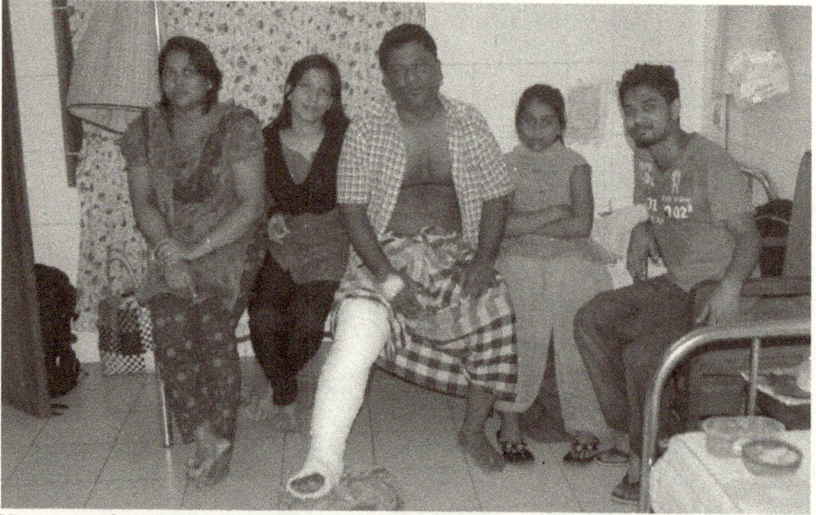

He was in there for a knee operation to correct an old injury.

All in all, my stay was blessed by brother Monir and his family. He took away any loneliness and his wife and his children filled it with laughter and conversation. I miss them very much but have lost contact with them after returning back to the UK. Their uncle is also in this picture who was the person running around for them and ensuring that all the meals were there on time and so on.

Sent email: 13

Sunday 23rd of May 2010

Hi Bruce,

It's been a while and its literally taken me this length of time to find a Doctor who has knowledge of vasculitus .

I have been directed to a Rheumatologist working for the Bangladesh Government Hospital in Dhaka. He also has a private clinic.

His name is: Dr Minhaj Rahim Choudhury MBBS, FCPS, DTCD, FACT(USA), Fellow Rheumatology England) Rheumatology, Chest & Medicine Specialist & Associate Professor BSMMU, Dhaka.
Nothing in Bangladesh is Free - you pay for everything.
I told him about the base line test you told me, he obligated.
I had a x ray - that was clear, no visible signs of anything.

Blood test -

Haematological	Reference	Value
Haemoglobin	14.9 g/dl	M= 15.2 g/dl
Erythrocytic Sedimentation Rate (ESR)	42 mm in 1st hr	M, up to 20
White Blood Cell	14,000 / cumm.	4000-10000 / cumm
Platelet count	270,000 cumm.	150000 - 400000 / cumm
Red blood cell	4.78 million / cu mm	M= 4.7-6.1

Differential count

Neutrophils	76%	40-70%
Lymphocytes	20%	30-50%
Monocytes	02%	02-10%
eosinophils	02%	01-06%

basophiles	00%	<01-02%
PCV/HCT	47.9%	36-50%
MCV	100.2fl ·	92-9fl
MCH	31.2pg	29.5-2.5pg
MCHC	31.1 g/dl	33- 1.5 g/dl

Biochemical test Plasma Glucose Random	5.45 mmol/l	3.33-8.88 mmol/l
S. Alt (SGPT)	25.0 u/l	M-upto 42
S. creatinine	1.31 mg/dl	m-0.80-1.30

Sero-immunology CRP	<6 mg/l	<6mg/l

ANA Screening
Sample value

4.80	< 10.0 U/ml = neg	> 10.0 U/ml = pos

I am also waiting for the C & P ANCA tests.

Once I have the ANCA results then we will sit down and discuss the course of treatment. Sorry to bore [you] with the above stats but [you are]the only one who I have [to] put my trust in for information and directions. The results above are concerning me as there are various activities in the haematology and creatinine side. I doubt that I will be able to discuss these in detail individually with the doctor and what they mean for me.

Since my last email I have spots all over my head and visible across my forehead and sides. I also have a chest infection but the mucus doesn't seem to want to go away.

I have also told him about ECG & CT/MRI, we will discuss this with the ANCA result.FYI = it seems, there is also a Vasculitus Clinic in Dhaka.

By the way Bruce, Do you have stats on how many Bangladeshi or Asian Vasculitus sufferers there are?

Would like me to send details of the other Doctors in Dhaka and the clinics for your database.

Email received: 11

Hello, Mayar..
It sounds as if you have a physician who will be able to be
effective in treating you. I certainly hope so. Interesting
that there seems to be a vasculitus clinic in Dhaka.

Thanks for the lab test results. I'm not medically trained, so
some of the lab results don't mean much unless I look them
up. I'll comment on what I think I know.

Elevated ESR just means inflammation somewhere in the
body… in your case, probably from the WG, and if you weren't
on Prednisalone, it might be higher. Or it could be elevated
due to your chest "infection". Elevated Neutrophils are
common with WG.

Your creatinine of 1.31 is so borderline that it's not possible to
say if your kidneys are affected or not. Watch that closely.
With WG in the early stages, blood and urine tests should be
rather frequent, at least weekly at the start. As you're on
Prednisalone, it may be making the creatinine measurement
look a bit better than if you weren't on the medication and with
treatment, the frequency of lab work may be safe at more than
weekly intervals.

The CRP upper limit of less than 6 mg/litre may be the older
CRP standard. The new standard in the U.S. is a "high
sensitivity CRP" (same test, but with the upper limit one tenth
of what it was before, that is, 1 mg/litre vs. former 10 mg/litre).
So it's possible that your 6 mg/litre could be six times the new
U.S. standard of 0.1, but I can't know that as I don't know the
practices in Bangladesh labs. I believe that being on
Prednisalone will elevate your blood glucose. An ANA result
in the normal range is common for WG. ANCA is a good test,
but better if supplemented with anti-PR3 and anti-MPO tests.
Some labs do all three if any one of the three is ordered.

It's likely that your spots could be acne, a common result of
being on prednisone. Your "chest infection" might be just that,
or might be a result of WG activity. My 2 cm nodule in one
lung didn't show on x-ray but did on CT scan.

I have no stats on the number of WG or other vasculitus patients in Bangladesh. Perhaps the Vasculitus Foundation (VF) at http://www.vasculitisfoundation.org has some info. I don't run a database of vasculitus clinics/centres, but quote the ones listed by the VF at their web page http://www.vasculitisfoundation.org/vasculitismedicalinst itutions

So I suggest you provide any info on Bangladesh physicians experienced in treating vasculitus to the VF or any Bangladesh Vasculitus Clinics/Centers. You can email them at VF@vasculitisfoundation.org

Good luck with your treatment under Dr. Choudhury. Let me know how things are going.

Regards, Bruce (WG '97)

Sent Email: 14

Saturday 24th of July 2010

Hi Bruce,

How are you? I hope you are well. It's been a while. This may become a long email.

About six weeks ago I had similar problem as my left eye, in my right eye; so I increased my Prednisalone to 50mg but soon after reduced to 40mg as I was experiencing discomfort, once I reduced it to 40mg the discomfort was gone.

I managed to see the Rheumatologist who admitted me to hospital and had the following tests done:

Blood test - ANA and the result was 9.10, in May 2010 the result was 4.8 so that's up. What does that mean?

C ANCA - negative (but it was positive in May 2010)
P ANCA - negative (but it was positive in May 2010)
Digital Chest X - nothing- lungs and heart normal
CT scan of the chest - nothing seen - lungs and heart is normal
MRI of my right eye nothing was notice -
Angiography of my both eyes - no vasculitus or lumps visible.
-

Even though most of the test came negative - ANA has increased; following symptoms persist & linger:

Pain in the right eye, Pain in the region of my right temple - between the skin and skull- mild throbbing pain that runs up to the top of my skull.

Dry chesty - hacking cough - when I do cough out, I find it difficult to breath back in - it's as if when I exhale (it's like a deflated balloon stuck together) especially at night I sometime wake up gagging for air (frightening)

Physical discomfort of my right lungs.

My skin tone is changing around my face and my hands, my chest hairs gone white.
I have macula oedema in the left eye as a result of the initial flare. I also have hearing problem- hearing reduction in my left ear.

Spots & acne in my forehead, face and palpitations
blood pressures increased 140/90 and higher
Slight soreness in my right nostril

The Dr could not determine the next course of action as a result of the tests. Personally I will need to get second opinion as the medical profession is full of "floors", however the rheumatologist is reputable as he is recognised as one of the top three doctors in the country.

He is with the view that he can't do anything until I am tapered off Prednisalone, then I need to retested and see what is the situation with me. I have already started tapering myself and am experiencing various discomforts, from joint clicking and popping, discomfort under my lower rib cage and mental block - and when I stand I'm having to think for long moments (pauses).

The Dr wants to put me on Cyclophosphamide - I have Googled this and I am not happy with the effects of this. I am seeking your guidance and advice on this medicine- to me it's a suicide pill. Under the situation and condition is in-appropriate to take this medicine - is this the only medicine that I can take or is there others - Imuran and others.

Since I left the hospital - this has been on my mind - a pill that will guarantee me cancer.

It's quite possible that I don't know what is really happening with me. It is also clear that I don't have an overview of my life with Wegener's and in the long run.

How long can I hold off before I need to take the - Cyclophosphamide - or the alternatives - at what stage?

Its quite clear that the WG is working its way - as it initially

started in the left eye, then the right arm and now the right eye - where next?
I need to keep an eye on my kidney? and follow up on the bloods tests. According to the physical tests it appears I'm well but according to the blood test - there's something?
I have also changed my diet - I am consuming regularly fresh pineapple, garlic, coriander and chillies, onions, oranges and other seasonal fruits that are available here in Bangladesh.

I am consuming seasonal greens; but the heat diminishes my salt level - realised this when I started getting cramps in my hands. (the heat and the pineapple are the culprit)

I wait for your reply.
Mayar Akash

At this point getting the doctor's opinion put me at another crossroads. I was alone, no one to talk to, who I would feel understood the situation that I was in. I had my chaperone with me who was from Bangladesh but with the village mentality, alien to this disease.

There was no-one reputable that we were aware of that I could get a second opinion from. I was in a foreign country, where I was not fluent in the language and people from my region of the country are part and parcel of thousands of people packed in like sardines in a tin.

This information sent my head spiralling. All I kept thinking was that I did not want to put myself into further harm's way than where I was with my health. I would rather wait and see what became of the condition I was in.

Received email: 12

Hello, Mayar.

You give me credit for more medical knowledge and judgment than is deserved. I'm only a WG patient of some 12 years.

You asked, **"1**. Blood test - ANA and the result was 9.10, in may 2010 the result was 4.8 so that's up. What does that mean?"

ANA according to one source, "Antibodies to nuclear constituents form in SLE (>90% of untreated cases) and other autoimmune diseases. Low tier ANAs occur in 5-15% of normal, especially in older females.". So a positive ANA means it's likely something autoimmune is going on, but is unspecific as to what that might be.

Likewise, you stated, **"2**. C cANCA - negative (but it was positive in May 2010)", and, **"3**. P anca - negative (but it was positive in May 2010)"

As you've been on Prednisalone for some time, that will make C-ANCA and P-ANCA test results more normal than without the medication, so your negative ANCAs may be false negatives. Also, regarding autoimmune vasculitides (AVs), these can sometimes be active with negative ANCAs, so they're not good measures of disease activity in general. They serve best as helping diagnose some AVs.

You stated, **"4**. Digital Chest X - nothing- lungs and heart normal", and **"5**. CT scan of the chest - nothing seen - lungs and heart is normal". You don't say whether the CT scan was a "high-resolution" scan or an ordinary CT scan. Sometimes things show up on a HR scan that don't show on the usual CT scan.

You stated, **"6**. MRI of my right eye nothing was notice - ". That's good. I don't know what vasculitides (including WG) might show on an MRI of the eye. I do know that pseudotumors behind the eye have been identified, but whether by CT scan or MRI, I don't recall.

You stated, "7. Angiography of my both eyes - no vasculitus or lumps visible." Excellent.

You listed your condition as having "[the] following symptoms persist & linger". I have numbered these for easy reference.

Pain in the right eye

Pain in the region of my right temple - between the skin and skull- mild throbbing pain that runs up to the top of my skull.

Dry chesty - hacking cough - when I do cough out, I find it difficult to breath back in - it's as if when I exhale (it's like a deflated balloon stuck together) especially at night I sometime wake up gagging for air (frightening)

- Physical discomfort of my right lungs
- My skin tone is changing around my face and my hands, my chest hairs gone white
- I have macula oedema in the left eye as a result of the initial flare
- I also have hearing problem- hearing reduction in my left ear.
- Spots & acne in my forehead and face
- palpitations
- blood pressures increased 140/90 and higher
- Slight soreness in my right nostril

The first two of these symptoms are of considerable concern, the eye pain and the pain in the region or your right temple pain running to the top of the skull. These can be symptoms of giant cell arthritis (GCA), also known as temporal arthritis (TA), another autoimmune vasculitus. If that's what you have, it is a medically very serious condition. It's possible your initial diagnosis of WG as an autoimmune vasculitus was correct about being vasculitus, but perhaps incorrect about being WG. IMPORTANT, see my comment below about getting off Prednisalone.

Your #3 symptom could the result of sinus drainage though I would have expected you to know that if your sinuses really are draining that much. The dry cough implies no infection to speak of, but possibly vasculitus damage. Waking up gasping for air could be sleep apnoea, but along with the difficulty breathing in, sounds much more like tracheal stenosis, a narrowing of the trachea due sometimes to WG (but can be from other causes). That can be identified by endoscopic exam of the trachea.

Your symptom#4, the physical discomfort from your right lung, could be something as simple as pleurisy, or else something unrelated to vasculitus.

About symptom#5, changes in skin tone, could these possible be due to the Prednisalone which generally causes facial bloating?

Symptoms#6 and 7 are unfortunate. I assume you have an ophthalmologist checking to see the macular oedema in the left eye doesn't worsen. Hearing can be due to fluid in the middle ear. If that's the cause, it could be infection, or effusion from tissues affected by vasculitus. Hearing may improve with effective treatment of the underlying cause.

Symptom#8 - Spots and acne are common with use of Prednisalone. After being off a time, the acne will likely clear and the spots may fade.

Symptom#9 - palpitations (of the heart, I assume) concerns me as autoimmune vasculatures can sometimes due damage to the heart that can be largely without overt symptoms. An evaluation by a cardiologist would be a good idea. An ultrasound of the heart might help reveal problems, but there are many other tests involved in testing for cardiac damage of which I have no knowledge.

Symptom#10 is common with autoimmune vasculitides. The damage to blood vessels impedes flow and raises the pressure. It might come down with effective treatment, but I don't know the likelihood of that happening.

Symptom #11 could be the result of many things, a lesion from WG, a viral infection.. I've no idea what the cause might be. If it worsens, surely your physician should know about it.

You mention additional symptoms after lowering your Prednisalone dose as, "... joint clicking and popping, discomfort under my lower rib cage and metal block ...". (I assume you meant "mental" block, not "metal" block). I have no particular comments other than roving joint pain is common when reducing Prednisalone. Those usually disappear in a few days. The mental confusion while on high dosage Prednisalone is common and usually disappears after one has been off it for a time.

While it's true that occasionally a physician will take a patient off medications to see the true state of things, I think you have to be very careful about possible GCA. When you reduce your Prednisalone, should you experience any sudden changes in vision, seek IMMEDIATE medical attention as vision can be lost temporarily, or permanently if not treated with high dosage Prednisalone. The emergency department (or whatever it's called), should be told you suspect giant cell arthritis/temporal arthritis and that high dosage Prednisalone may be required IMMEDIATELY if the cause of the change in vision is GCA/TA. I don't know if you have GCA, but you must be very quick to react if your vision suddenly changes and those are due to GCA.

Are you perhaps using urine dip sticks to test for protein and blood? It's a moderately inexpensive way to check without having to go through the lab testing. If you're having frequent tests of blood and urine, the dipsticks might be unnecessary. If the urine testing is very infrequent, then the urine dipsticks would be a good idea.

I think your move to a diet of fresh fruits and vegetables is a move toward a less inflammatory diet.

Best wishes for finding the kind of treatment you need to restore your health.

Bruce (WG '97)

(From: blades49456 <blades49456@sbcglobal.net To: Mayar Akash <mayarakash@yahoo.com, Sent: Sat, July 24, 2010 9:19:48 PM, Subject: Re: Hello Bruce - to take or not to take - Cyclophosphamide)

Sent email: 15

<u>25th July 2010</u>

Hi Bruce,

Thank you for taking the time to respond back to my email. I appreciate it very much.

I have notes GCA/TA and I will look into that.

I am still unclear about taking or going onto Cyclophosphamide - I just don't want to be carted onto it by the Dr's.

What information can you provide me?

Is it my only option? what alternatives do I have?

Mayar Akash.

Sent email: 16

Hi Bruce,

How are you? It's been a while since my last email.

I'm still in Bangladesh and plan to go back to [the] UK in May/June 2011.

After returning from Dhaka seeing the doctors, I have reduced taking the Prednisalone; however, I did not return to see the doctors.

I think I hit a point, where I had gone down to 1 pill, 5mg - but noticed burry vision and dizzy, visual disorientation. As a result I increased my dose - recently its come to a point where I've noticed in the increase of pain under my ribs. As a result I've been checking my urine, the protein marker is increase to ++, and as a result I've increased my dose to 25mg, soon as I increased the dose, I had some comfort, however, after first few day, in the last day and a half, I'm getting discomfort in my right side.

Along with the discomfort under my ribs, I've been having palpitations and what feels like a murmur. I have also notice my joints clicking and pain in my lower back, knee and my right arm.

I've also noticed the feeling of blocked/fullness of vein above my right temple and the usual sleeplessness. So far I've been self medicating and don't have reliable or knowledgeable Dr. I plan to have a protein check, along with ECG, it is difficult to get local "ANCA" test, I have to travel to Dhaka.

what other test would you suggest? I am concerned about weakening/damaging my heart, kidney and bones.

Thanking you in Advance
Mayar Akash

Received email: 13

Bruce sent me a link for more information.

1995 information
Bruce (WG '97)
Heather Smith wrote:
Fascinating news in the NY Times today!
http://www.nytimes.com/1995/09/15/us/scientists-discover-gene-that-causes-inflammation.html

(From: blades49456 <blader49456@yahoo.com, To: wgdiscussion@yahoogroups.com,
Sent: Tue, January 18, 2011 12:46:08 AM, Subject: Re: [wgdiscussion] Scientists
Discover Gene That Causes Inflammation)

Received email: 14

Hello, Mayar..

I think you have good reason to be concerned about several things.

Medicating yourself for an autoimmune vasculitus is asking for trouble. True, sometimes a short course of prednisone or Prednisalone will get things quiet again, but that's not happened for you. You simply must take very seriously your diagnosis and symptoms. All the information needed to effectively treat you is available from reliable sources on the internet and so there's no reasons for an English-speaking physician in Bangladesh not to search out and find that information and treat you.

If your only treatment has been prednisone (or Prednisalone) for the last year, and you yet have symptoms, then it's very evident the steroid hasn't been adequate to control whatever vasculitus you have. On top of that, prednisone or other glucocorticoids will cause bone loss over time. Some of that can be prevented by supplemental vitamin D and calcium and a bone-loss inhibiting medication such as alendronate, Boniva, or Forteo or similar. But the objective in the U.S. now (in most specialized vasculitus clinics) is to get the patient off steroids in about 3 months or so by using one of the immunosuppressive meds or biological meds (very expensive) or intravenous immunoglobulin G, or plasmapheresis. Regardless of what method is used, you need to find a way to keep steroid usage to a minimum (5 mg/day or less), and even then you likely will need the calcium and vitamin D supplement and probably the bone-loss prevention medication.

Some of your symptoms sound a bit like polyarteritis nodosa, some like WG, and some like giant cell arthritis (GCA).

I don't know why you're in Bangladesh where effective treatment seems unavailable. if you can go to the U.K., or any of the major European countries, you should be able to find the expert care you need

To summarize your current symptoms:
1 Blurry vision
2 Dizziness and visual disorientation (not sure what the latter means)
3 Pain under ribs
4 Increase of protein in urine
5 Discomfort on right side
6 Palpitations and possible murmur
7 Joints clicking
8 Pain in lower back, knee, and rt. arm
9 Fullness/blockage of right temple vein
10 Sleeplessness

There's many possible reasons for each of these, but certainly an autoimmune vasculitus and prednisone can account for some of them if not all
Numbers 7 and 8 could be due to osteoporosis or osteopenia caused by the long term steroid use. Prednisone also explains #10, and possibly #1.

Of particular concern are no's 4, 6, and 9. Number 4 implies damage to kidneys. Number 6 suggest possible heart damage. Number 9 could be WG or could be another autoimmune vasculitus, Giant Cell Arthritis or GCA (also known as temporal arthritis). All three are of serious concern and should be addressed by medical professionals well acquainted with WG and similar autoimmune vasculitides.

If possible you should not extend you prednisone use. However, if you have no adequate medical care then perhaps to guard against blindness, heart damage, and kidney damage, you may need to continue taking high doses of prednisone (up to 60 mg/day for example). Yet your first objective should be to get the immune system controlled by immunosuppressives such as Cytoxan or biological agents such as Rituximab, etc.

If you truly have WG or a similar autoimmune vasculitus, then you simply must find knowledgeable and experienced medical help (not me!).

Let me remind you that Wegener's Granulomatosis until a few decades ago was invariably fatal within two years if untreated.

Your months on prednisone have protected you to some degree without solving the underlying problem that seems to be Wegener's Granulomatosis. But if you don't get effective treatment, you'll suffer the consequences of bone loss due to prednisone and likely continued damage to blood vessels and organs.

Best wishes for finding more effective treatment.

Bruce (WG '97).

(From: blades49456 <blades49456@sbcglobal.net To: mayarakash@yahoo.com, Sent: Thu, January 20, 2011 6:18:25 AM Subject: Re: [wgdiscussion] Re: Still in Bangladesh)

Sent email: 17

Saturday 22 January 2011

Thank you, Bruce.

This was my final email to Bruce and the Wegener's group. These emails were instrumental in my guidance and life.

I would like to express my gratitude to Bruce, God bless you, wherever you may be, Amen.

*NB: *Please note that the information in the email section was written in 2010 and will be out of date. Please check all links and information for updates on-line. The knowledge about Wegener's Granulomatosis is always being discovered.*

The intended purpose for inclusion of the emails are to give the reader firsthand account of what happened to me and what I did when there was no information of groups readily available in United Kingdom in 2010.

One Way

In Bangladesh, I found myself accepting the fact that I had made a one-way trip and I was never going to return back to anywhere else, other than to die and get buried there. So, having a Muslim upbringing, I would not get to go to Makkah as is obligatory for a Muslim to do so. I consoled myself and then decided to make visiting all the Mazaars of three hundred and sixty Auwliyah, my pilgrimage. I firmed up my belief and determination with an open mind and set off with my parents' blessings to Dorga.

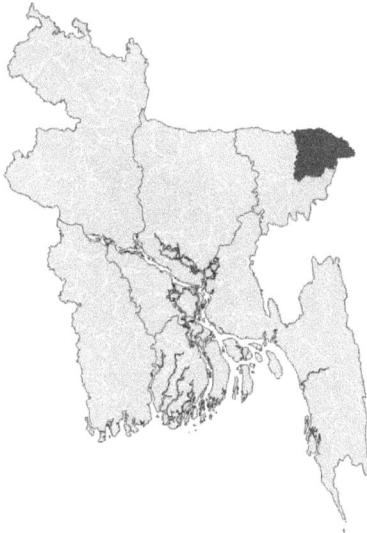

My life in Bangladesh took a different turn as a result of my predicaments and the choices that I was making. I was focused on my primarily being in my parents' care. I became that child again while I became their physical and visual support and backbone. They were not without their 'flesh and blood' in a country where 'Londonis' get sucked dry of their resources by all and, in particular, by predators, when they see weakness and vulnerability – it's like the vulture's circle.

[A 'Londoni' is someone who resides in London, England, United Kingdom; similarly, Bedeshi, Probashi are Bangladeshis who live outside Bangladesh, anywhere in the world and return to the country, they are referred to as Bedeshi and Probashi, NRB: Non Resident Bangladeshi]

Once I found my feet, I was communicating via emails with Bruce and during the day I was fulfilling my "Bucket List" as well as putting a care-plan together for myself.

My list was to visit the shrines in Bangladesh, which entailed travelling the country and taking in the sights, the people and the customs; I would also be photographing and documenting these visits.

The care-plan was to get familiar with the systems and process, locate the professional people that I would need to support me. I outline this further on in the book.

Throughout this period I was very humbled and appreciative of my parents and my siblings. I was fragile, vulnerable and was in lamentative state of being but I pursued my bucket list as a way of distraction.

So when I got to the Dorga, I visited the office to get official consent/permission to photograph the Mazaar. I was asked for the purpose of my photography and was I representing any media companies, by the late Kobir Ahmed. He then told me to go the district office and get permission and come back.

So that upset me and set me back on how I had planned it. He had just instructed me to take a very exhaustive run-around, where I would have to jump through bureaucratic hoops, pay fees and most certainly bribes, I would be taken for a "jackass" by the people I was going to have to go to.

I left the office and decided that I would go and photograph the Mazaar anyway and I did. I was not going to let anyone stop me but, having taken the pictures, I did not feel happy or content with myself. Little did we know then that Mr Kobir (in the picture) was going to die of pneumonia only a few weeks' later.

On leaving the Dorga that day, I decided to purchase some books on three hundred and sixty Auwliyahs as a reference guide and visit them.

For support, I needed to set up a communications system which would allow me to be up-to-date. I had my computer shipped out to me and I purchased a USB modem that allowed me unlimited data at a cost of ten English pounds a month, which was equivalent to a thousand Bangladeshi takas. I continued communicating online to my 'light in the dark'.

I returned back to the Dorga. By this time, I had visited one hundred and fifty Mazaars throughout Sylhet, had designed and produced business cards, purchased a domain name and had opened a website. The website was up and running with the pictures of the sites.

Spiritual

In pursuit of this spiritual enlightenment, I had my parents' blessing and their trusted vehicle and drivers. However, this only covered the main roads but not the paddy fields, muddy tracks and the waterways.

While the weather was reasonably consistent, it did differ from region to region like anywhere else in the world.

I had not realised then what the physical travelling would turn out to be; the discipline I was implementing in my life at that time. I had a sense of purpose to visit these places; researching, planning and executing the plan of action.

The travelling to and fro from each destination allowed me to reflect while I sat in the confines of the passenger seat, with the 'revving' of the engine, the music, the passing of other vehicles outside; all the scenic views of the landscape just visually stimulated my mind. As a photographer, I love scenery, lush green, palm trees and the colours. The other aspect was the heat. The sun was constant and it was firmly on me, my arms, my face - it was the whole package.

The journey was working on me in so many ways that I was not qualified to understand.
- Venturing out not knowing what to expect, so in anticipation, expectation;
- Then the heat of the sun and the engine, hot and clammy;
- Then the vibration of the engine and the centrifugal force from the vehicle's movement and coupled with the bumps from the road surfaces, from smooth to the rough;
- Then the breeze from opening the window or the door depending on where I was sitting in the vehicle;
- The constant and ever-changing lush green scenes of the paddy fields and the villages, those beetle nut trees to the banana trees; the greenery that is so easy on my eyes;
- The resolve to accomplish this planned action's execution;
- The reception at the sites;
- The fact that I was photographing each visit;
- That I was documenting for the purpose of using to show and educate others; the sense of purpose was my reason why;
- A whole range of transitions taking place with me simultaneously.

Map of the Sylhet district of Bangladesh.

During the times that I travelled to these places, I encountered so many difference experiences and challenges. It was a real eye-opener; there was nothing that I could not be open to.

Rain water-filled pot holes, an excruciating ride.

Walking through the rice fields

Walking over makeshift ramps

Muddy village tracks

I was always very wary of snakes but have to admit that I did not encounter any during my travels.

Slippery mud –the path waterlogged after the rain.

Water-logged terrains

Mayar Akash

Rugged, mud terrains

Through the forest

Negotiating the narrow paths.

Crossing the rail lines

Crossing a river via a ferry

Tea estates

Climbing the steps to the top of the hill in a deep forest. A steep climb.

Crossing the river on boats, Khalique, my chaperone, assisting the boat owner.

Looking back, there was a lot of travelling and it was a good experience. I look back at it with fond memories. Everything was new -a new challenge.

Boarding connecting boat ferries.

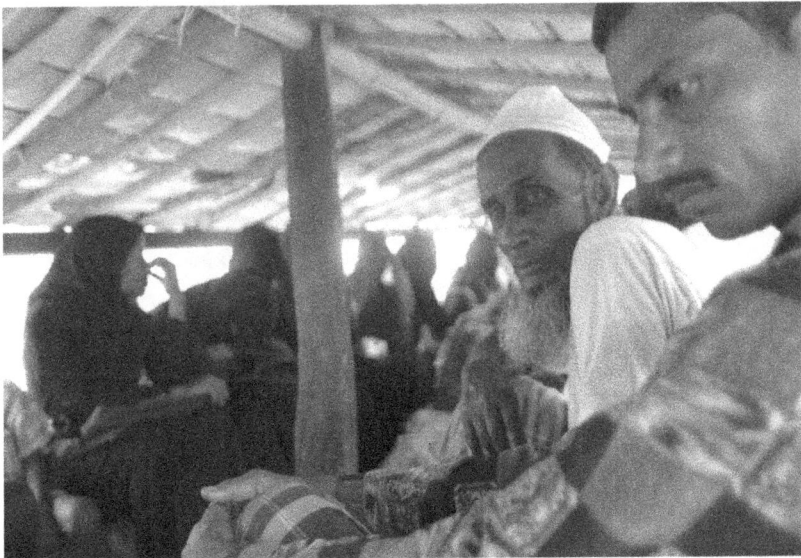

A few of the people that I was privileged to have on my journey to my destinations.

Hazrat Shahjalal's Shrine

I went back to the office again and there I found Mr Kobir Ahmed once more when I presented myself again. I gave him my card and told him what I had done up until that point.

He looked at me and said "You are possessed" (Phagoleh doriliseh) and then summoned his son (Sonnet) and that was that. He took me over to Moutowalli Amanullah for me to ask him for permission to take pictures of the Mazaar. He was sitting in the courtyard, as pictured. The encounter was brief and he gave permission for me to take few pictures to the chaperone.

I went into the Mazaar and started taking pictures. When the watchman there objected, my chaperone informed him that I had permission. I took pictures until I was content and I felt vindicated and also felt a bit smug for having been given permission to take pictures. I felt proud knowing that I was only the second person to be allowed, in the history of the Dorga, to take pictures of the shrine/Mazaar.

This set me on my way to go on and visit over two hundred and fifty sites and amassed seeing and photographing five hundred phirs, and Auwliyahs in Sylhet, Moulivi bazaar and Dhaka.

I now had a wealth of knowledge and photographs to produce a number of books. As a photographer, I love to show my photos and I have taken many thousands. So, I am producing a book with a lot of photos, just as if one is going through an album. There are many images that are so full of life, colour and depth that I feel it would be unfair not to include them.

I would have loved to put all of the pictures in but how long and big would the book be! In this book, you will see photos of the inside and outside of the Dorga and personal ones which I was given exclusive access to.

This one of Urus was his last but he was not to know that when I came into his life. I had taken a few shots of him and one that particularly sticks in my mind is where we were waiting in the cooking room, waiting around as they were getting organised and he called me over and handed me a ticket, a ticket to eat. This would be the last time I would see him, in the last few hours remaining of Urus before the akri (last) milad and fajar namaz.

Above image (This was the last time he saw me. Who was to know that in few weeks' time he would not be with us).

Mr Kobir died from pneumonia, fluid in his lungs, in hospital. Fortunately, I saw him in hospital where I handed over a CD to him with the photos that I had taken of the event.

He wanted to speak to me regarding the promotion of the event and its history. He believed that I would write it differently from that which had been written to date by others; I will reach an audience that others don't, the young British Bangladeshi and in English.

We parted with the understanding that after he recovered we would discuss about how best we could tell future generations of Sylhetis about the Sufi Saint of Sylhet. Unfortunately, that day never came. A couple days later, I got a call to say that he had passed away.

I went to his funeral and spent the day with the family. They looked after me well. I suppose attending the funeral was also character-building for me.

Pilgrimage

When I got over to Bangladesh I was on a one way trip and that I wasn't going anywhere else nor will I be able to finance it. That meant as a Muslim I was obligated to go to hajj, pilgrimage to Makkah, Saudi Arabia. I didn't have a source of income for myself and I did not make any arrangement nor did I have any financial asset.

So I substituted going to the shrines of the three hundred and sixty Auwliyahs in Bangladesh.

- Emotional
- Reconciliation
- Opening up

Spending time in our Mukam

Getting to them with the intention of reaching them, physically setting on foot, saying a prayer; making the intention to proceed with the choice made to visit all the shrines;

While there, lighting the candle to contemplate, reflect and soak in the atmosphere and the environment; allowing the mind to open up a little at a time; to take in and replenish the mind a little; absorbing the sense of history and aura that each place had.

While I was there, my eyes were soaking in the sights, my vision was as a starved community - looking and sucking it in while using the camera to click away, collecting a multitude of snapshots.

Just entering in the shrines was like dipping into water and each experience differed place to place; from hot water, to warmish water, to lukewarm water, to cold water. It must have been due to the time of the day.

Inside the shrine complex: white-tiled ground, tranquil and serene. It is clean to sit anywhere, preferably where you can get under the shade of the trees - the white bounces the heat back, so the place is even hotter.

There is no segregation in the courtyards but the women have their own prayer, wash and contemplation area and are not permitted in the enclosed shrine on top of the steps, this is for males only. As someone who had grown up in the East End of London within the conservativeness of my community there, it was a breath of fresh air and an eye-opener to see and experience men and women walking around without separation in a religious complex.

The Mazaar complex has a large pond full of medium snakefish, which the devotees and visitor feed with small fishes and other meat.

Inside the main enclosure at the top of the steps is the grave shrine, clean and tidy and revered. Devotees contemplate, offer prayers and seek blessings, making offerings while there of money, flower, candles and incense sticks.

Aromatic rosewater may also be sprinkled and the Holy Book, the Quran, may also be donated to the mosque within the shrine for others to read during their stay of contemplation.

I took this image with a fisheye lens, hence the arching-in at the sides.

In entering into the inner shrine of the Patron Sufi Saint of Sylhet, Hazrat Shah Jalal, you automatically receive a dose of serenity and tranquillity with all the aromas and fragrances of the rosewater and incense sticks. You see and feel the presence of people and their silent meditations and contemplations.

Because the place is kept so clean, this gives your mind complete relaxation, free from the worry about getting dirty, no apprehensions or inhibitions, just contemplation and the reverence to the saint.

My mind was in total calmness, as if someone had thrown a bucket of calmness over me. I sat in the corner and observed what was going on around me as well as taking some pictures to capture the scene, the setting.

Building Development

While I was there I also undertook duties to oversee some toilets being built on the top floor which had inadvertently become a major construction development in my parents' house.

It was my father's desire to see further development on the property which he had started. Doing this work while he was alive was helping to fulfil his lifelong ambition.

This building had been built in 1988 and, in my opinion, was need of modernising, so I started re-designing the building and circulating this out to the family for their input.

I was going to modernise it so that it would be in style for the next twenty to thirty years.

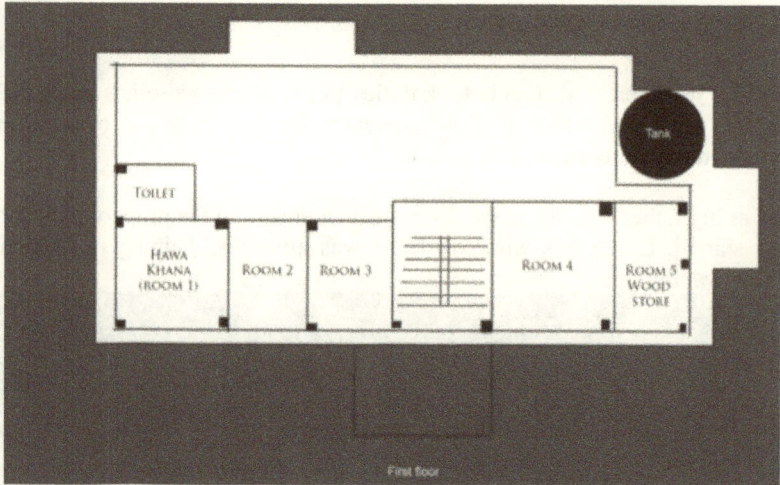

This gave me momentum and drive - something significant and major was happening to me, to my dynamics, with my parents, in particular my father and also with everyone else, the locals, the builders and so on.

Using my computer, I designed the façade and the room layouts. While the room layouts were finished as planned, the façade turned out differently. I was not there in Bangladesh to see the finishing of it but my elder brother saw it to its end. Sadly, our father had passed away by then and had not been able to see the completion of his dream. He died of cancer in the UK on the 20th March 2012.

01.12.2010: My father doing his daily walk around. Little did he know how much it would alter from his design; even though he did see parts of the design chiselled away.

A garage was included in the re-build, to keep vehicles. Much of the inside of the ground floor remains the same to when it was built in 1988. My parent's money provided most of the finance with some from my siblings but mainly from our eldest brother.

This is the final finish of the building with white walls, tinted green windows/glass with steel/chrome railings on top; and trims painted in light aqua blue.

This project occupied me for months, it kept me on my toes, with all the different aspects of it - finance, accounts, purchasing, designing, consulting, quality control, monitoring and other logistics such as paying the wages.

This would not be everyone's cup of tea and not everyone would have this kind of opportunity or facility to undertake something like this or half the things I was able to do while I was in Bangladesh with my parents. But this was my life journey and is about what these activities did for me and to me.

Doing this development made me feel good. I was doing something in the presence of my father, something he expected and desired and it was an accomplishment for me, an achievement - I felt important, I was in control, I was determining, deciding, delivering, and so on; this altered my mindset and outlook on what I was doing and doing before I died. I was making my father happy; I was happy that I was doing this and so on, one trigger after another. It was also a matter of local prestige; this is inherent in the life culture and community.

Returning back to United Kingdom.

Returning back to the UK was not in the plan, as I had seen this as one-way, accepting my fate - that I would fall ill and battle with the illness and then eventually die.

But, circumstances had other plans. I know I made many intentions and deep-rooted was the acceptance to my submission to God. With everything that was going on and happening in my head, heart and mind, the moment came when I took a very deep breath in and breath out and said to myself that I was ready -ready to meet my Maker.

With this acceptance came so much that I am still analysing what happened and what had made the change, or rather, made the Wegener's Granulomatosis disappear?

Like I said, I had accepted my circumstance and had accepted that I was ready to meet my Maker and throughout the process there were my prayers and inhibitions at work; discussing and negotiating terms, references and conditions and so on as one does, especially being the introspective person that I am.

Yet, this is the human part of me after I got back to the UK from Bangladesh. I started recalling and analysing my experiences, trying to understand what had contributed to the disease disappearing, when did the healing process start in the journey, could I identify any of the signs?

Looking back, I noticed that the test results done Dhaka in Bangladesh were negative. My lamenting had taken place before I went to Dhaka; my spiritual journey had taken place before going to Dhaka. It was only me trying to put a timeline to it all; to plot, map out the journey so that I could visualise it. That is just me.

I looked at everything I had done and made a list and then, after returning to the UK, I discovered through conversation about an motivational speaker who talks about how chemicals in our body rules our inner world. I also revisited some of the old knowledge that I had collected about the blood group types, positive mental attitude and knowledge from various books about how our emotions rule our lives and living too.

In the following pages, I have written about them and how, by looking deeper into them they had supported me in my recovery.

Positive Mental Attitude (PMA)

This positive mental attitude and health came about from getting involved in an on-line business and self-development which involves the "law of attraction". I had been unable to put it into action until I had the necessary tools to change my mind-set, to stop attracting bad health, to stop thinking about illness.

The second part to this 'changing to positive mind-set' came when I started to understand what was going on with me; for whatever mental reason, I was then able to control my mind to changing the thought pattern/process. This only occurred after I had become fed up with the aches and pains and feeling ill and having gone to the GP who then referred me to the consultants, I would then be told that there was nothing wrong with me - I was physically well with no signs of the disease or its conditions.

My lung is fine even though I still have asthma. My brain is fine; my heart is fine, even though I have a slightly-raised cholesterol level.

Through research we can find out more as we discover new and updated versions of science theories and discoveries. For me, I was able to understand that my immune system was poor, yet as a blood group 'O' person, the immune system should be over-active and in the WG case it was, but for everything else, such as general health, cold and 'flu, the body was breaking down all the time; I was always tired. So, once I had found out about the effects of zinc and Vitamin C and then later magnesium, I started taking separate supplements.

Minerals & supplements

Zinc

I now also understand that my immune system was weak because I didn't have the right amount of zinc mineral that my body needed. Once I added this as a mineral supplement, my cold and 'flu incidences reduced. I had fewer colds, runny nose, burn-outs and bronchitis. I also educated myself to think more positively and see myself in positive health.

Magnesium

I also added a magnesium supplement to counteract the lethargy and tiredness I felt much of the time, even after good night's sleep and eating a healthy diet.

Testosterone

I also understood from my physician that the flabbiness around my mid-section was related to high oestrogen and low testosterone levels.

Vitamin C

I added 500mg Vitamin C, which did not make much of a difference. Then I increased the dosage to 1500mg but this made me feel unwell, I felt uncomfortable, as if I was coming down with a temperature. So I reduced the dose down to 1000mg capsules. This along with the zinc was making me feel better. However, I was still feeling tired and lethargic during midday and at the end of the day.

I then started researching into why this was so and this lead on to many possible reasons. However, what I was able to deduce from the information 'out there' was that physically you may feel tired when you have an underactive adrenaline gland. I am no expert but I knew what I was feeling like and how my life was, so that was when I introduced magnesium into my supplements.

Soon after I started taking the magnesium I began to notice that I was not feeling tired or lethargic. I also learned that the magnesium was also helping my body to produce testosterone. The lack of testosterone in my body was also contributing to my body and my figure. Due to the level of testosterone level in my body I had 'belly flab' and 'man boobs'.

So after coming back and looking at what I had learnt, revisiting the past knowledge took me to another level to reflect and implement new systems and approaches to my well being.

Blood Group

"We, as humans, know much about the world around us but we know little about our inside."

Along this journey I have encountered many different aspects of my life from the "I don't have long to live", and "my life has been cut short" perspective.

I looked into my blood group in order to find out what my blood group was. I donated blood and they processed it and told me what group I was. The first time round I forgot what it was and lived for many years thinking I was blood group 'A'.

Then after getting through Wegener's Granulomatosis and finding out that my blood was clear, I donated blood again and this time it was confirmed in print that I was blood group 'O' and not 'A'. OMG!

This changed the complete scene, the landscape of my life. I had already been looking into blood groups and came across a myriad of information, as one does when searching on-line. I had come across the following books by Dr Peter J. D'Adamo with Catherine Whitney. The books were "Live Right 4 your type" and "Eat Right 4 Your Type".

Dr Peter J. D'Adamo is an eminent naturopathic physician and researcher with a wide international following.

Here I discovered so much about myself, it was unreal. This was the moment when I began to fill in the blanks - the missing jigsaw pieces in my life.

Blood group 'O', the hunter-gatherer, is the oldest blood group. And more to my discovery was this group has an inherent disposition with our immune system: they flare up. "I'll be damned".

As an 'O', I am prone to autoimmune diseases, if I do not look after myself.

According to this book, I had been eating the wrong food and doing wrong activities - lumbered with high cholesterol levels, because despite having a small and slim build, a 'hunter-gatherer' person stores fat in their blood and not obesely on the outside.

Learning about the effects of a blood group and how food affects the person is so over- powering! It is also fascinating to learn how different foods react when we eat them.

This is a 'must read' for everyone but especially for people with auto-immune diseases. It will allow you to understand or eliminate reasons/causes for your state of being.

The following books are great to start with.

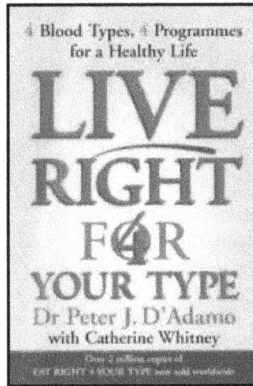

"So I lived my life eating the wrong foods, the wrong lifestyle and so on and then to be halted in life and be told that I had to take a pill to have cancer in order to deal with the disease that I was inflicted with".

Healing Powers of...

After I had returned from Bangladesh, I came across a book called the "Healing Journey" by Matthew Manning. The title compelled me to pick it up and read it.

The book covers powerful ways to beat cancer and other serious illnesses. I came across the 'healing power of' section and was further captivated as it encompassed what I had done in Bangladesh but had not seen my actions that way.

- The healing power of laughter
- The healing power of hope
- The healing power of optimism
- The healing power of social support
- The healing power of love
- Healing power of forgiveness
- Power of belief

Each title I read was like a playback of what I did but categorising them within the titles.

Having returned back to the UK without the disease and attributing it to the spiritual journey, reading this was validating all that I had gone through – it opened the doors of insight as to what had taken place; along Simon Sinek's chemical and biological reaction.

There had been a systematic healing process that had taken place inside me that had altered my health state to cure me.

- There was laughter around my mother
- There was hope in my thoughts
- There was optimism in my drive
- There was social support from the place and people who were around me in Bangladesh
- There was love, love from my mother and love from my father, and I had received like a child

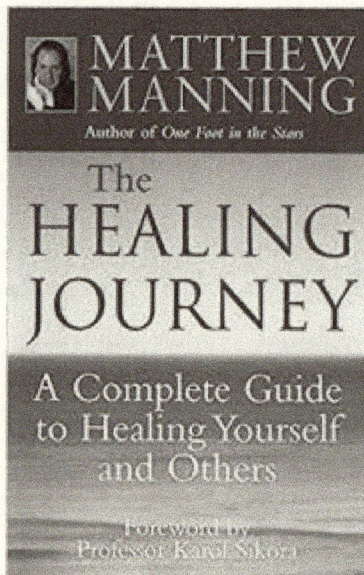

- There was letting go of the past, letting in the dumping of bulk negative thoughts, feelings and old wounds

- There was my faith focused on God and the shedding of earthly thoughts and doings as I was getting ready to make my Maker.

On reflection, all I can recollect is that I had somehow connected myself to the healing portal and all its healing powers had come into action and they had done their magic, with a little help from Prednisalone.

Therapies

The Healing Journey made me reflect back, simply scanning what had happened during my stay, revisiting all that I had done knowingly and unknowingly, looking at it in-depth to see what could have cured my Wegener's Granulomatosis.

Colour therapy

– The uplift I got from seeing lush green vegetation and the palm tree, the vibrant blue sky and myriad of colours of the fauna.

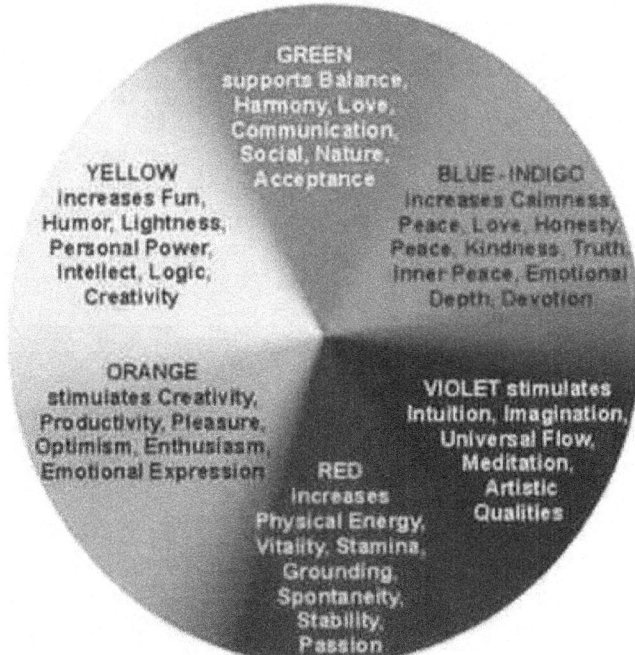

GREEN
supports Balance,
Harmony, Love,
Communication,
Social, Nature,
Acceptance

YELLOW
Increases Fun,
Humor, Lightness,
Personal Power,
Intellect, Logic,
Creativity

BLUE-INDIGO
Increases Calmness,
Peace, Love, Honesty,
Peace, Kindness, Truth,
Inner Peace, Emotional
Depth, Devotion

ORANGE
stimulates Creativity,
Productivity, Pleasure,
Optimism, Enthusiasm,
Emotional Expression

RED
Increases
Physical Energy,
Vitality, Stamina,
Grounding,
Spontaneity,
Stability,
Passion

VIOLET stimulates
Intuition, Imagination,
Universal Flow,
Meditation,
Artistic
Qualities

Image capture from the internet

Aroma therapy
– The change of mood from the smells, aroma and fragrances from the land, cattle, water, plants, trees, scents from the incense sticks and perfumes and author.

Gardening therapy
– Number of effects from this, the physical aspect such as digging, hoeing, sifting, cutting, and so on; exposure to the sun, the planting, watering.

Physical exertion therapy
– Regular gardening, lifting of pots, digging, sifting, carrying of water, carrying my camera, rucksack and walking.

Heat therapy
– My body was hot 24/7, I was clammy, sweaty and was hydrating myself on a regular basis.

Sun therapy
– The sun was basting down on me most of the time, when I was gardening, travelling, on location of tombs. The sun was on my head and body and to the exposed face, neck, arms and feet. I must have had plenty of vitamin D & E.

Relaxation therapy
– When I was not working I was relaxing, sitting with my parents, when I travelled to locations, sitting in the garden admiring the beauty and the work, sitting up on the rooftop of the house under the tree shade looking down into the garden and out to the surroundings. Where possible, I rested until I felt rested; I lounged around at first in various parts of the villa complex, on the veranda, on the roof, out in the porch, by the pond.

Natures sound therapy
– During my time in Bangladesh, I was surrounded by Nature's sounds, of birds, crickets, gracos, wind, the rain, rustle of leaves in the breeze, the white noise of the fan.

Pond life therapy
– Sitting beside the pond where there were fish swimming on the surface, the green of the water, the light reflecting off it, little ripples from the breeze, the trees, the mango tree, the beetle nut tree, the guava tree, the bamboo fence, the flowers, the birds, the butterflies, the dragon and damsel flies; the

kingfisher, the lizard - there was so much going, it was such a pleasure, the serenity, tranquillity, peace, calmness and feeling of contentment, the constant sighing, relaxing and recharging of my inside.

Koi fish in the pond.

Photographing therapy

– I was enjoying photographing all aspects of my time in Bangladesh. Photography is a passion of mine and I was swimming in it. I was high on my passion.

Doing what you want therapy
– I was relieved and went through release, had release of hang-ups and inhibitions of holding back.

Tender Loving Care therapy
– While I was there, I received TLC from my parents - my mum and especially my dad. What I received from my dad touched me in so many ways. I felt so humbled, that he could do that when our relationship had been strained for so many years.

Appreciation therapy
– While pursuing my resolve to visit the shrines of the saints – people around me and those that got to know me, showed and expressed their appreciation and I appreciated them for the commitment and support to me and my goal.

Reaching out therapy
– My parents received me and so did the spirits on my spiritual journey and quest.

Writing therapy
– While I was there I did not keep a journal but I did write frequently about whatever was bugging me. I wrote poems, written accounts, recollected my thoughts, replaying scenes with my pen, having question and answer

sessions, understanding the reasons and my reactions and actions; what was it that made me react and take action the way I did? I used pen and paper as the third person in many conversations that I had with myself. This helped to unload the mind's intricate web which was like a spiral of thinking, inhibitions and re-thinking.

Green therapy

– this is the feelings, emotion and moods that I experienced while in the country. I was happy, content, satisfied with the colour green that enveloped me there. I simply love colour and loved the different shades of green.

Serenity of the village life

Warm breeze therapy
– This was a real pleasure having the warm breeze running through my hair and over my face, neck, arms and feet. This gave me comfort and pleasure - it was like bathing in power.

Insects and small creatures' therapy
– Watching them doing their 'thing' was a joy to watch, marvel at God's creatures, witness God's plan in action. The colour of these creatures was also mesmerising and discovering or seeing a creature for the first time was a complete joy.

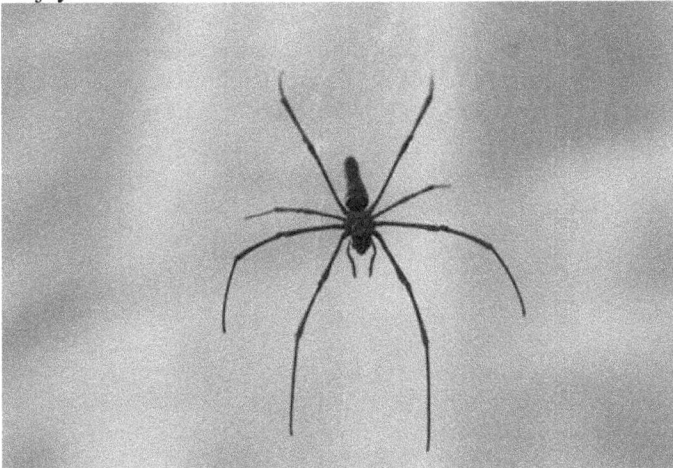

Spending time with both parents therapy
– Was soul nurturing for me, realising and accepting that I may have spent something like this time with them when I was four or five years old (maybe) because he would have been at work and I do not have a good memory of such times. So, the fact that this could have been the first time that I had such quality, priceless time with them is very precious to me.

Being needed therapy
– Even though I was there for my own reasons, I was still needed by both of my parents. My parents felt more comfortable and content with the knowledge that I was with them, that they had a son with them that people got to know that one of their children was with them and it acted almost as a deterrent for foes. They were happier and for me to witness this, made me happy within.

Caring therapy

– The time I was giving to all things around me, caring for my dad and mum, them looking out for me, tending to the gardens, tending to the fish in the pond and looking after the property,

Watching growing therapy

– Especially in the gardening section where I was planting seeds and saplings and then watching them grow, becoming lush, and the flowers blossoming, watching fruits, vegetables and flowers growing from month to month and season to season. I had the joy of seeing mangos, boroi, papaya, guava, coconut, jackfruit, other local fruits, vegetable okra, aubergine, radish, onions, mohilia shag, Edo, Lotta and the flowers all shades of roses, mehendi leaves, purple, magenta, red, white, yellow, pink flowers. Watching this new growth and its colours gave me joy within and uplifted my mood and soul.

Travelling therapy

– This was one that gave me anticipations, expectation, exhilaration, challenge, meeting new people, spending eleven months there with my parents and travelling all over the Sylhet district and the capital city, Dhaka.

Accomplishing therapy

– During my time I did what I wanted, designed a garden, started applying the design and constructing it in the forecourt, decided that I would visit the shrines and visited two hundred and fifty of them, spend some pure, quality time with my parents, just them and me, all in a fragile state.

Took on building works while my dad was alive, which he wanted to see but on a small scale, bit by bit. I undertook researching about my ancestors as part of my family tree. Going around the family and talking about it and taking notes, and then adding this to the rest of the data collected.

Visiting the shrine therapy
- Knowing that I would draw attention where I was taking photographs and asking questions on location.

Lighting candles therapy
– This was a spiritual aspect of the journeys, lighting up candles, leaving a light for the spirits. Each time I lit candles I knew I was reaching out to the spirits, no one in particular but all those that were surrounding me and the area where I had lit them.

Praying at the sites therapy
– Each site that I had visited, about two hundred and fifty of them, I would say a little prayer or perform Salat if it was the Jamat time. This was my personal connection to God through the spirits around me. The silent contemplation, meditation and reaching out to the universe and connecting to God.

Touching people's lives therapy
– During my time in Bangladesh, I touched many peoples' lives as well as them touching mine. Of the people, some appreciated me, some felt for me and some enjoyed my company. So many different interactions had taken place, visiting all the shrines, for example, had caught people's attention and they had expressed that it was spirit-led; some appreciated my generosity and valued the gesture where the community neglected it/them.

Eating fresh fruits therapy
– During my time I was consuming fruits, especially mangos, boroi, coconut, papaya and citrus fruit from our trees in the yard. I was also enjoying fruits from the trees when visiting relatives. I particularly enjoyed pomelo fruit from my aunt's bari (place).

Sharing knowledge and experience therapy
– Having conversations with people who wanted to know about me and where I came from and what it is like and so on. Likewise, I was finding out about what they did and how they managed and also learning new knowledge of the saints from the locals.

143

Cold wash/shower therapy
– It became a routine to have a warm to cold shower and wash during the hot weather. The chill of the first jug of water, sending shivers up and down my spine and then the body adjusting to the temperature.

Planting sapling therapy
– This was about taking something from another plant and planting it and then watching it grow and transform into another plant, to witness the miracle of growth.

Feeling safe therapy
– I felt safe because my parents were protecting me, they were informing me of the climate

Feeling content therapy
– This feeling interconnected with all that was happening and going around within my immediate circle – the feeling of settlement, fullness, satisfaction and appreciation; being humble and filled with humility.

Making friends and acquaintances therapy
– When I was in the hospital at Dhaka, I made friends with people of all ages and we shared some humbling moments.

Dr Mahbub, a family member of Monir's family, who is a dentist working in the hospital.

Dr Mahbub and his wife and his friends invited me for lunch, I was very humbled and my respect and appreciation goes out to them. It was a well laid-out lunch with many delicious dishes.

I got to meet all these lovely people in Dhaka during my stay in the hospital for my assessment. They gave me much appreciation and respect and hosted me in their homes with lovely, delicious home-cooked meals.

Here is a list of feelings and emotions that I experienced during my journey of recovery.

Joys   Value
Elations   Happiness
Release   Laughter
Mesmerising   Satisfaction
Surprise   Gratitude
Pride   Shock
Excitement   Fulfilment
Respect

I have put the above list together having had the chance to reflect and also learning something different from listening to Simon Sinek's 'YouTube' videos when he explains about the four chemicals that we have in our body that shape how we feel.

This triggered a number of thoughts about what types of experiences I may have had while in Bangladesh that helped me. The C ANCA test in London was negative and I was told by the GP and the consultant at the Moorfield's Eye Hospital that I no longer had WG.

I did not know what to do; my relief was muffled, as it had been a lonely journey that I had taken. I had not shared my inner most thoughts with anyone about my predicaments.

What you will have found in the beginning of the book is that I had been putting together my life from the perspective of all my woes and mishaps - to build a case where depression contributed towards me getting the vasculitus disease, based on the information and knowledge that was available then in 2010.

Yet now in 2020, the latest knowledge about the cause of the disease points to it being bacteria-led. This knowledge does not change the facts about all that had happened to me and, as a direct consequence of those situations and circumstances had led me to sleep on a dirty basement floor where I could have breathed in certain bacteria while sleeping only four inches off the floor.

Could it have been an office on the basement floor of a community centre of a Bangladeshi organisation that had caused my disease - its heavy traffic and minimal cleanliness along with the tiled carpet, dampness and moulds?

What is clear is that both situation and circumstance were facts of my life. However, I am still none the wiser, despite knowing all of this information from 2010 up until the present day, I am still curious as to what caused my attack.

Having gone through it all and acquiring all this information and knowledge that I have included in this book, has given me a new 'window' into my life so that I can re-examine it. This is also a post-recovery treatment to analyse, re-assess and re-evaluate the actions and processes taken during the period of my illness.

I am so grateful to have come across Simon Sinek; learning about my blood type and DNA. This knowledge has taken me to different level of awareness about myself and I only wish that I had been made to learn this sort of thing in my childhood along with my religious and cultural teachings and activities. I would then have known that my immune system is sensitive and prone to autoimmune disorders and that I am a highly-tuned individual needing regimented 'looking-after.' I would have been aware of the types of foods I should eat, the physical activities I should do and so on.

I believe learning about who we are and what we are, how we are meant to be, how we have been set, made and so on would stand us in much better stead. The sad thing about it is that this knowledge and information is readily available in this modern time, with the internet at our finger tips.

STRENGTHS	WEAKNESSES	MEDICAL RISKS	DIET PROFILE	WEIGHT LOSS KEY	SUPPLEMENTS	EXERCISE REGIMEN
Hardy digestive tract	Intolerant to new dietary environment	Blood clotting disorders	High protein. Meat eaters	Avoid: wheat corn kidney beans navy beans lentils cabbage Brussels sprouts cauliflower mustard greens	Vitamin B vitamin K calcium Iodine licorice kelp	Intense physical exercise, such as: *aerobics *martial arts *contact sports *running
Strong immune system	Inflammatory conditions		Meat fish vegetables fruit			
Natural defenses against infections	Immune system can be overactive and attack itself	Immune diseases— arthritis Low thyroid production	Limited: grains, beans, legumes			
System designed for efficient metabolism and preservation of nutrients		Ulcers Allergies	Aids: kelp seafood salt liver red meat kale spinach broccoli			

Image of the table with list for the O group, from book featured on page 128

We can learn so much of ourselves through the knowledge that is already available to us:

Blood Type - Gives us insight to what blood group we belong to and for that blood group what is best for us - to eat, to work, to exercise, what illness and other things relating to our type, we may be prone to.

DNA - gives us our physical pedigree, what our body is made up of and what qualities we have within. This information also gives greater in-depth knowledge, subject to what knowledge you seek.

Personality test - Alchemy - this is what I call the "firmware", your firmware, what you have as your core programme.

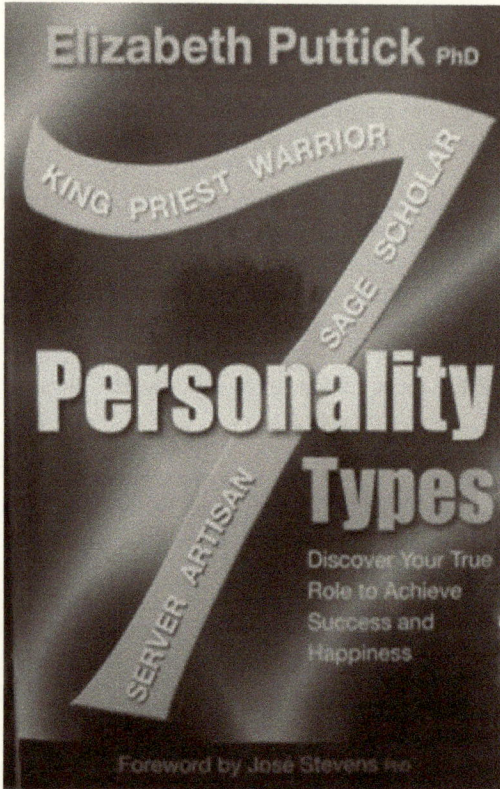

Your astrology - what is your star sign - knowing your star sign, whether you are a Capricorn or a Gemini, gives you an insight to who you are and how you will conduct yourself.

The Chinese astrology - this also helps you to determine your characteristics, how you live and conduct yourself. For me, the Chinese element's sign determines your inner-self and strength.

I am sure you have heard the one about the ears - the bigger the ears the better listener you are and so on. Similarly, most other parts are true, too - your hands, your eyes, your lips, your feet and your body shape. Although this knowledge is readily available, it is not widely known or commonly used, nor is it given the recognition it deserves.

Knowing even half of this information about yourself will stop much time-wasting and heartache and will make you a stronger and well-balanced person with a strong sense of autonomy. This knowledge will aid you in many aspects of your life - life choices and decisions; in careers and in love.

I am not and do not advocate anyone to go to people and become their 'cash cow' or fall victim in any way. This is for self-learning in your own time and pace, grasping what you are good for, what you do well naturally and that this blue-print came with your birth - it is another level of living.

Coming back to the central point in highlighting this, is that this knowledge has helped me to cut through a lot of life's emotional and mental grime. I have stripped away the layers that were hurting me. This knowledge has allowed me to identify why I do what I do, the way I do it, the way I think things, what I value and what I don't; my likes and dislikes. What I will defend and what I will fight for - for what I will lay down my life for. Why I react to people, in what they say, in how they say it, why I would want to understand, be objective, and so on.

These are the things that Buddha and many other learned men and women went into the wilderness for - to find themselves. Once they had found themselves, they brought forward the knowledge for us to do the same but there is no need for us to go into the wilderness to do that but the tranquillity and serenity of it is mind-opening.

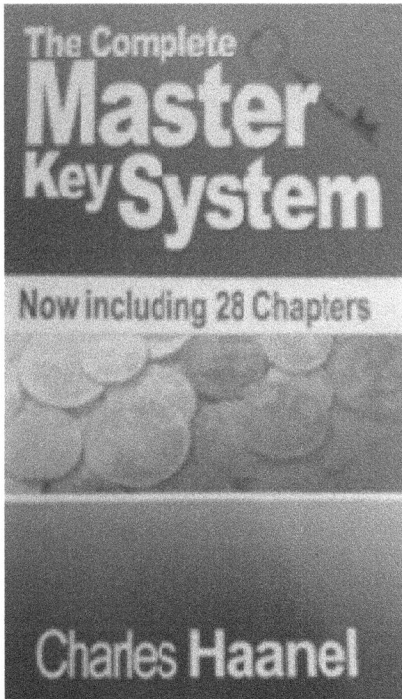

I now know, reflecting back, that I was doing all of this in Bangladesh with the disease in me but I was not aware of it. And this is the thing, the self-verification and validation, what had happened and the action you took at the time. It is only afterwards, when you come across all this knowledge and suddenly, everything begins to fit like jigsaw pieces– that is when you learn that there is a greater truth out there.

The master key system book is also another source of knowledge that gives insight into our inner world - Things that you cannot quite 'put your finger on' or 'hit the nail on the head'.

This book goes through many social challenges and anyone who is serious about self-development and wanting to know about their own potential and worth, should read this. This book made me aware and more alert to my inner-being. It sheds light on what is literally happening within us every second of our lives- that which we do not see, understand or even realise is happening.

Simon Sinek

Coming back to therapies, in 2016, I joined a local fitness gym as I wanted to tone up and exercise with weights under instruction with a personal trainer. During this time, my fitness instructor mentioned about a speaker who he listened to; someone who spoke about how our actions trigger various chemicals in us that makes us feel good. So I followed this up and sat and watched a couple of his videos on YouTube. Simon Sinek is well known in the 'giant's land' such as Apple, Dell, Intel, Microsoft and so on and some of the viewings of his videos are in their millions - he is definitely someone to watch.

> *Simon Sinek (1973) is a leadership guru, professor at Columbia University, founder of SinekPartners (Corporate Refocusing) and author. He is best known for popularizing the concept of "the golden circle" and to "Start With Why". Simon Sinek is also an adjunct staff member of the RAND Corporation.*

I watched the video where he talks about how we feel when each of the four chemicals is triggered, and is the basis of the actions we make and take. This made me think about the outcome of my medical condition. Other than divine and spiritual intervention, could there have been chemical intervention also? Simon Sinek does a breakdown of the chemicals that are in our body and what their function is; how they interact and how they make us feel.
(https://www.youtube.com/watch?v=ReRcHdeUG9Y&t=1173s)

Endorphins – are neurotransmitters which transmit electrical signals within the nervous systems. They are released when we hurt ourselves or suffer pain.

Dopamine – this is a neurotransmitter which transmits signals in between the nerve cells (neurones) in the brain. It becomes activated when something good happens unexpectedly, such as the sudden availability of food. *(www.psychologytoday.com/blog/mouse-man/200904/what-is-dopamine)*

Serotonin – is a neurotransmitter and is mainly found in the brain, bowels and blood platelets. It transmits impulses between nerve cells, regulating cyclic body processes and contributing to wellbeing and happiness and is regarded as chemical that is responsible for maintaining mood balance. *(www.medicalnewstoday.com/kc/serotonin-facts-232248)*

The Oxytocin – is a hormone that is made in the hypothalamus which is found in the brain. It is transported to, and then secreted by, the pituitary gland, which is located at the base of the brain.

In chemistry, Oxytocin is classed as a noapeptide (a peptide containing nine amino acids), while its biological classification is as a neurpeptide. it acts both as a hormone and as a brain neurotransmitter. *(www.medicalnewstoday.com/articles/275795.php)*

It is very possible that all of these chemicals where being 'injected' into my system, and giving my insides a real cleansing - flushing out the cortisol and others unpleasant things which had accumulated over the years.

This knowledge helped me gain a basic understanding of my healing journey from a biological view and this, I believe, may well have been the key to my recovery.

On reflection, Simon Sinek's explanation of how these hormones work certainly gave me further insight into learning and acquiring knowledge about myself.

Travelling to Bangladesh, making this journey, had got my system 'going' with dopamine. As I recall my journey and look back at how I was met at the airport by my mother, I remember the sense of relief, the feeling of safety as my mother received me; the overwhelming sense that I had arrived and this continued to happen throughout my stay in Bangladesh for nearly a year.

As well as the dopamine for achieving the journey, there would also have been the release of serotonin from the welcome my mother had given me and also Oxytocin because of the trust, love and hug I received from her, and the smile that lit up her face when she saw me -the mother and child 'lock of the eyes' that settled me; that gave me a re-assuring feeling, the protectiveness of it.

I must have received this dose all over again when I arrived at our home where my father was waiting - it must be the serotonin that makes you sigh.

After I had returned from Bangladesh, I started to reflect on the trip - the planning that I did, the journeys that I made, the decisions I took, the actions that

I executed, the people that I met, the people who valued me, the people that I was able to help and the joy I was able to facilitate and so much more as I have listed in this book.

This is a diagram that I came across on Facebook, which puts it nicely.

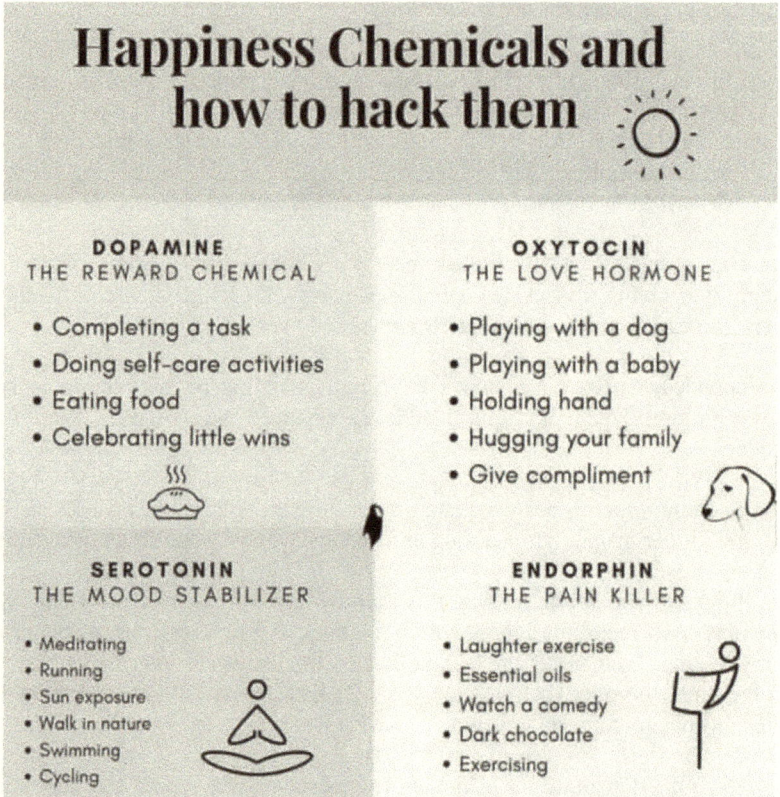

Happiness Chemicals and how to hack them

DOPAMINE
THE REWARD CHEMICAL

- Completing a task
- Doing self-care activities
- Eating food
- Celebrating little wins

OXYTOCIN
THE LOVE HORMONE

- Playing with a dog
- Playing with a baby
- Holding hand
- Hugging your family
- Give compliment

SEROTONIN
THE MOOD STABILIZER

- Meditating
- Running
- Sun exposure
- Walk in nature
- Swimming
- Cycling

ENDORPHIN
THE PAIN KILLER

- Laughter exercise
- Essential oils
- Watch a comedy
- Dark chocolate
- Exercising

Joe Bangles Hicks, Dyspraxia Support Group, 25 September at 12:21, Saw this on a karate group I follow. How to hack happiness.

The chemical Acetylcholine

I learnt something new from this clip on Facebook from the BBC. The chemical, 'Acetylcholine'. A little insight into my way of dealing with the world I live in.

https://www.facebook.com/BBCOne/videos/277346466911012[23-7-2020]

This leads on from what Simon Sinek had brought to light about the four chemicals and how they shape us -how this chemical acetylcholine counters dopamine.

I loved the clip as it gives the best description me. Here is a transcript of part of the scientific theory from the clip:

> There are two important chemicals found in all brains. Dopamine and acetylcholine. Dopamine is like a hit of energy when we take risks or meet new people - and it makes extroverts feel great. But introverts are more sensitive to dopamine and get quickly over-stimulated.
>
> That's why we prefer the more slow-burn feeling we get when our brains release acetylcholine.

That happens when we concentrate, read or focus our minds. It makes us introverts feel relaxed, alert and content but it barely registers with extroverts.

Of course, like anything, it's a sliding scale. You can lean one way, or another - or be a bit of both - known as an ambivert.

This was a great find for me. While this does not define my life completely, it certainly throws some light on it. I certainly enjoy that time alone and have had the relaxed, alert and content feelings many times.

This process had been happening for a while but I had not recognised it, particularly in my early life when there was so much turmoil in my personal circumstances along with physical head trauma I had received.

These nuggets of information gave me real insight about myself. Now I can look back and analyse, but back then, I would not have known what to do with all this information. It is the journey that conditions one; introspection is another layer to a person like me - inherent and solemnly working away within us.

It would have been of great benefit to me earlier in my life if this information had been available. It could have facilitated my decision-making, help to inform my choices, remedy or re-align my reactions and responses that went on to be damaging and detrimental to me, my life, and my well-being.

Gratitude and Appreciation

Although I have returned to the UK and knowing what I know now - that I am clear of the disease that had been within me, I am grounded with the knowledge that I am where I am, mentally well because of my spiritual pursuit, yet still inhibitions have been bombarding me with all that I have mentioned already in the book.

It was this grounding that made me value and appreciate the journey I had made - one of the inner voice, my spiritual one, this spiritual trip had been my venture, starting from my own Mukam of my ancestors, Shah Mullah Mubarak Shahab of my father's clan and Shah Shikondor Shahab of my mother's clan and then our local one. This was the beginning of the spiritual growth that propelled me to go on to the main leader of the all the Sufi saints in Bangladesh and in Sylhet city, the district where I lived.

As I made these trips before my medical visit to Dhaka, I found myself getting stronger with each visit to each shrine, amassing to two hundred and fifty different locations around Sylhet and Dhaka and about five hundred individuals, saints, phirs and fakirs. With every step of this journey I felt myself getting stronger, my fear and inhibitions melting away. I felt grounded and ready to 'look down the barrel of the gun' being presented before me. I had gained the necessary emotional and mental strength.

To this day, I attributed this change to the spiritual journey I made, and that journey started with the saints and as a result, I made it a point to pay my respects to the saints of Bangladesh starting at the top by writing about them and publishing books to take the saints to the people.

I have so far written five books, discussing the saints and the traditions. I have also created a website covering all the sites I visited and taken photos of.

The website is www.mazaar.org.uk

155

Wegener's Granulomatosis

The Cause

It looks like the knowledge about this disease has progressed quite a bit since 2010.

This is what I had to deal with.

No one knows exactly what causes Granulomatosis with polyangitis. It appears to develop after an infection or other inflammation-causing event triggers an **abnormal** reaction from your immune system. This reaction can lead to **inflamed, constricted** blood vessels and harmful **inflammatory** tissue masses (granulomas).22 Dec 2015

[www.mayoclinic.org/diseases-conditions/granulomatosis-with...causes/dxc-20167228]

If this is now the case, then I can recall sleeping in a basement office, where I remember coughing from breathing in the dust and other environmental allergens - from the carpet, the damp, the mildew and germs and bacteria brought in by people using the facility.

So up until more recently, I believed my illness was depression-led as extensively listed.

Granulomatosis with polyangitis can occur at any age. It most often affects people between the ages of forty to sixty five.

"It happened to me at thirty eight years old, earlier than then thought".

Name change

We hope that patients will in future be diagnosed with "ANCA-associated vasculitus" instead of "Wegener's disease". Those who have the opportunity to read this text can help to make it widely known, so that situations like that do not continue to happen i.e. that is, to honour war criminals by attributing their names to important discoveries in medicine. In a recently published article, the American College of Rheumatology, the European League Against Rheumatism and the American Society of Nephrology have proposed an alternative name for "Wegener's Granulomatosis": "Granulomatosis with polyangiitis".

Nazi past and changes in disease names: the Wegener's disease case

This is what is known about the history of the disease.

"An inflammation of the arteries and veins of the lungs, facial sinuses, and kidneys had been identified as a specific type of chronic granulomatous inflammation. In 1937, Friedrich Wegener, a pathologist in Berlin, described the disease, which became known as "Wegener's Granulomatosis," an autoimmune disorder, in which antibodies attack their host.

Despite the suspicion of his participation and collaboration with the Nazi Medicine, the allies released Wegener due to lack of evidence that he had taken part in Hitlerism. However, subsequent and more recent investigations, conducted by Eric Matteson, a rheumatologist at one of the most prestigious American medical centres called the Mayo Clinic, have shown that Wegener was actually a dedicated Nazi, who affiliated with the Nazi Party months **before** Hitler rose to power - differently from other physicians, who had to affiliate with Nazism to continue to practice medicine.

Wegener worked as a military pathologist at Lodz, Poland, where the first Jewish ghetto was installed, housing over two hundred and fifty thousand Jews. According to Dr. Matteson, Friedrich Wegener was a dedicated Nazi - it was impossible for him to not have known what was happening. Wegener died in 1990, at the age of 83 years, after having received several honours from the British Thoracic Society and the American Thoracic Society.[4]

Medical societies have begun a campaign to rename "Wegener's Granulomatosis" to "ANCA-associated granulomatous vasculitus" (ANCA - anti-Neutrophils cytoplasmic antibody test). The American Lung Association used to have a prize named after Wegener, for young pulmonologists, but has rescinded it. One year before his death (1989), Wegener was awarded a Master Clinician prize by the American College of Chest Physicians, which has also been rescinded. In my scientific production, I have included some studies on that disease, and I also want their titles to be modified. Much progress has been made in the treatment of that disease but it can have a fatal outcome when response to treatment fails.

Morton Aaron Scheinberg, PhD [http://www.scielo.br/scielo.php?pid=S0482-50042012000200014&script=sci_arttext&tlng=en]

This is the British version:

Following information is from the http://www.vasculitis.org.uk site as was 25.12.2017 (The PDF Format).

Granulomatosis with Polyangiitis (GPA) previously known as Wegener's Granulomatosis

Reviewed and revised by
Dr Chetan Mukhtyar MBBS, MSc, MD, FRCP, FRCPE
Consultant Rheumatologist Norfolk and Norwich University Hospital

June 2016

Change of nomenclature
The name of this vasculitus disease was officially changed from Wegener's Granulomatosis (WG) to Granulomatosis with Polyangiitis (GPA) in 2011.

Throughout this descriptive section it will be referred to as GPA.

What is Granulomatosis with Polyangiitis?
GPA is a type of primary systemic ANCA associated vasculitus (AAV). It is the most common type of this group of vasculitus diseases. It usually affects the kidneys, lungs, ears, nose and sinuses. GPA is characterised by inflammation of the small blood vessels including the capillaries.

Who are affected?
It is most common in middle-aged and elderly people but can affect young adults and children. It affects men and women, equally.

What is the aetiology (cause)?
The cause of GPA is not yet known. Some research suggests that GPA may be triggered by exposure to **silica** or to infection with **staphylococcus aureus** bacteria though this is not proven.

The ANCA antibodies found in most patients with GPA play a role in causing the inflammation of the blood vessels by activating some types of white blood cell. The ANCA antibodies attach to the neutrophils in the blood causing activation. This makes the neutrophils attach to the blood vessel wall and cause damage by releasing the chemicals that are usually used to fight infection. It is not understood why patients develop ANCA antibodies.

What are the symptoms?
The disease can present itself in very different ways in different people depending on the severity of it and the organs involved. It is not uncommon for patients to have had mild symptoms for months or even years before seeing a doctor at all.

Common general symptoms include tiredness, loss of appetite and aching muscles and joints.

It is very common for GPA to affect the ears, nose and sinuses, causing a blocked nose with some bleeding, crusts and blood clots. Deafness is also very common due to inflammation in the ears, as is pain in the face or headaches due to sinus inflammation. The eyes can also be involved. In some patients, the kidneys can be severely affected which leads patients to go to a doctor with symptoms of kidney disease.

Other common symptoms include:
• **Lungs** - breathlessness, wheezing, a dry cough or coughing-up blood
• **Skin** - rashes, ulcers, and necrosis (death of tissue)
• **Eyes** - red (blood shot) eyes, painful, dry or gritty eyes, visual loss or other changes in vision
• **Nerves** - loss of sensation, weakness, unusual painful symptoms in the hands and feet (hotness, pins and needles or "electric shocks") and in rare cases, paralysis or stroke
• **Bowels** - Diarrhoea, bleeding and abdominal pain.

Diagnosis
As in other types of vasculitus there is no single test which confirms the diagnosis. The diagnosis will depend on the doctor recognising the pattern of symptoms and examination-findings. Blood tests usually show evidence of inflammation. The blood tests for ANCA are usually positive which help support the diagnosis but are not specific for GPA or vasculitus. A biopsy of the affected organ (if readily accessible) may be helpful in confirming the diagnosis. For example, brain or eye involvement are best not biopsied, whereas kidney or nose involvement are easily biopsied.

GPA can often present with non-specific symptoms of unwellness, fever, malaise and may mimic infections, making it difficult to diagnose. If the lungs are primarily affected, it is not uncommon for the disease to be mistaken for lung cancer, pneumonia or TB.

Treatment

Cyclophosphamide in combination with glucocorticoids (steroids) is the mainstay of treatment in most cases. In specific circumstances, methotrexate or mycophenolate mofetil may be substituted for cyclophosphamide. For patients in reproductive ages and for other situations where there are contraindications to the use of cyclophosphamide, your doctor may choose to use Rituximab. If the disease is very severe, large doses of methylprednisolone or plasmapheresis (plasma exchange) may also be given. When the disease becomes 'quiet', less toxic drugs are used to keep it under control which include: azathioprine, methotrexate and mycophenolate mofetil.

In patients where initial treatment was with Rituximab, it may be continued in a smaller dose at four to six-monthly intervals. The Prednisalone will be tapered slowly over time with a view to coming off the steroid completely. In some cases, this may not be possible and a low-dose of Prednisalone may have to be continued long-term. The treatment will be continued for at least two years after the onset of remission after which it may be appropriate to start reducing it in certain cases.

For information on plasma exchange:
• Plasma exchange or plasmapheresis

Drugs and Side effects

For information on the main drugs prescribed for GPA, see:
• Azathioprine
• Cyclophosphamide
• Methotrexate
• Mycophenolate Mofetil (Cellcept)
• Rituximab
• Steroids

For information on other drugs used in the treatment of vasculitis, see Glossary of drugs and side effects.

Prognosis

The overall prognosis in GPA depends on the amount of damage that has occurred to organs, especially the kidneys, when the disease was active. Relapses are common and can occur in up to 40% of patients, two years after remission. The doctor would have to change the immunosuppressive treatment in the event of a relapse, although in some situations it may be possible to simply increase or commence a small dose of Prednisalone (steroids).

Key Points
- GPA is the most common type of this group of vasculitus diseases
- The disease may be present for months or years before a diagnosis is made
- Treatment depends on the severity of the disease
- The disease commonly relapses after the initial treatment.

The American version

Granulomatosis with polyangiitis

According to the Mayo clinic website, the following information is how they view the illness.

Granulomatosis with polyangiitis is an uncommon disorder that causes inflammation of the blood vessels in your nose, sinuses, throat, lungs and kidneys.

Granulomatosis with polyangiitis, formerly called Wegener's Granulomatosis, is one of a group of blood vessel disorders called vasculitis. It slows blood flow to some of your organs. The affected tissues may develop areas of inflammation called granulomas, which sometimes affect how these organs work.

Early diagnosis and treatment of Granulomatosis with polyangiitis may lead to a full recovery. Without treatment, Granulomatosis with polyangiitis can be fatal.

Symptoms
Signs and symptoms of Granulomatosis with polyangiitis may develop suddenly or over several months. The first warning signs usually involve areas of your respiratory tract, such as your sinuses, throat or lungs. The condition of people with this disease often worsens rapidly, affecting blood vessels and the organs they supply, such as the kidneys.

Signs and symptoms of Granulomatosis with polyangiitis may include:
- Runny nose, stuffiness, sinus infections and nose-bleeds
- Coughing, sometimes with bloody phlegm
- Shortness of breath or wheezing
- Fever
- Fatigue and general aches and pains
- Numbness in your limbs, fingers or toes
- Weight loss
- Blood in urine (hematuria)
- Skin sores or bruising

- Eye redness, burning or pain
- Ear infections

For some people, the disease affects only the lungs. When the kidneys are affected, you may not notice any early warning signs. But blood and urine tests can detect the problem. Without treatment, kidney failure and anaemia often occur.

When to see a doctor
See your doctor if you have a runny nose that does not respond to over-the-counter cold medicines, especially if it's accompanied by nosebleeds and pus-like material, coughing up blood, or other warning signs of Granulomatosis with polyangiitis. Because this disease can get worse quickly, early diagnosis is key to getting effective treatment.

Causes
No one knows exactly what causes Granulomatosis with polyangiitis. It appears to develop after an infection or other inflammation-causing event triggers an abnormal reaction from your immune system.

This reaction can lead to inflamed, constricted blood vessels and harmful inflammatory tissue masses (granulomas). Granulomas can destroy normal tissue and narrowed blood vessels reduce the amount of blood and oxygen that reaches your body's tissues and organs.

Risk factors
Granulomatosis with polyangitis can occur at any age. It most often affects people between the ages of forty and sixty five.

Complications
Besides affecting your nose, throat and lungs, Granulomatosis with polyangitis may affect your skin, eyes, ears, kidneys, heart and other organs. Complications may include:
- Hearing loss
- Skin scarring
- Heart disease
- Kidney damage
- A loss of height in the bridge of the nose (saddling) caused by weakened cartilage
- Deep vein thrombosis
Source:

https://www.mayoclinic.org/diseases-conditions/granulomatosis-with-polyangiitis/symptoms-causes/syc-20351088

Links from 2010

In Canada
Canada - Rebecca MacDonald Centre for Arthritis & Autoimmune Disease Mt. Sinai Hospital, Toronto, CA
http://www.mountsinai.on.ca/care/rmcad/contact-us

In United Kingdom
U.K. - Addenbrooke's Hospital – Cambridge
http://www.addenbrookes.org.uk/serv/clin/renal/services/vasculitis_lupus.html

U.K. - University of Birmingham
http://www.crf.bham.ac.uk/

London, England, UK
Perhaps soon to have a vasculitus multi-discipline centre, Hammersmith Hospital in London, U.K.
See http://www.nhs.uk/ServiceDirectories/Pages/hospital.aspx?id=RYJ03&v=0
Contact Drs. Professor Charles Pusey, Renal Medicine; Alan Salama, Renal Medicine; Philip Ind, Respiratory Physician; Dr. Guri Sandhu ENT.

Email
VOICE4VASCULITIS@yahoogroups.co.uk
VF@vasculitisfoundation.org
wgdiscussion@yahoogroups.com
Vincent Fernandes has set up a London Support Group:
0208-8660602, vincentf51@hotmail.com
Oxfordshire vasculitus support group <oxonvsg@hotmail.com>

In France
France: Groupe Français d'Etude des Vascularites
http://www.vasculitis.org/

In Germany
Germany: Rheuma-Klinik Bad Bramstedt and University of Luebeck
http://www.rheuma-zentrum.de/

In USA

U.S.A. - Johns Hopkins Vasculitus Centre   (Baltimore, Maryland)
http://vasculitis.med.jhu.edu/
U.S.A. - Cleveland Clinic Centre for Vasculitus (Cleveland, Ohio)
http://my.clevelandclinic.org/rheumatology_immunology/vasculitis_center/defau
lt.aspx
U.S.A. - Boston University - Vasculitus Centre   (Boston, Massachusetts)
http://rarediseasesnetwork.epi.usf.edu/vcrc/centers/boston.htm
U.S.A. - Emory Vasculitus clinic-Atlanta
http://www.medicine.emory.edu/divisions/lowance_center/patient%20care/make
_an_appt.cfm
U.S.A. - Univ. of Alabama, Birmingham
http://www.health.uab.edu/11263/TKC/12286/
U.S.A. - Univ. of California in Los Angeles
http://healthsciences.ucla.edu/healthcare/institution/groups-
detail?group_id=12753
U.S.A. - Univ. of California at Davis
http://www.ucdmc.ucdavis.edu/cliniclocations/specialtycare/specialties/rheumato
logy.html
U.S.A. - Univ. of California in San Francisco
http://medicine.ucsf.edu/rheum/
U.S.A. - Univ. of Utah [Select "Rheumatology" and then Dr. Curry L. Koening
M.D.,M.S.
http://medicine.utah.edu/internalmedicine/rheumatology/vasculitiscenter.htm
 U.S.A. - Pennsylvania State University Vasculitus Centre
http://www.hmc.psu.edu/rheumatology/aservices/vasculitis.htm

1995 Information

 http://www.nytimes.com/1995/09/15/us/scientists-discover-gene-that-causes-
inflammation.html

This Was The Information In 2010

NEW TO WEGENER'S GRANULOMATOSIS
(or to a Wegener's Granulomatosis email group?)

Hello, and welcome to one of the Wegener's Granulomatosis email groups. It is good that you have found this group as the many members can give lots of support, information, and experience. Cyndi in CA created the current wgdiscussion group when the original wg-discussion group was discontinued. Later, a parents4wegeners group and a wegeners-teens-only were added. It is good you are already a member so you can be in contact with other WG patients.

This "canned" email that I usually send to newly diagnosed WG patients is expanded in my web page on WG (See address at the end). Here, I just try to hit the essential points.

I address this directly to you because it is lengthy and because most other email members have already seen information such as that below. I am not medically trained, so NOTHING I say here or anywhere is to be taken as medical advice. All medical problems, symptoms, concerns and questions should be referred to appropriately licensed, medical professionals.

GETTING CONNECTED
If you have not already done so, you can join the Vasculitus Foundation, International (VF) formerly the Wegener's Granulomatosis Association (WGA), for $25/yr in the U.S. (U.S. $30 to foreign addresses) and receive their bi-monthly newsletter. If you cannot afford a membership, VF will subscribe you to their newsletter at no cost.

Contact them regarding membership and the patient packet at their web page at http://vasculitisfoundation.org or email to vf@vasculitisfoundation.org or phone 1 800-277-9474. Outside the U.S. telephone 816-436-8211. You can download a pdf file with information for new patients at http://www.vasculitisfoundation.org/node/1921

There are some support groups around the U.S. that meet. A list of contacts for various states in the U.S. is on the VF web page at http://www.vasculitisfoundation.org/support/domestic
For international contacts,
see http://www.vasculitisfoundation.org/support/international
The contact for your area or state, province or country can help you get in touch with other WG patients in your vicinity and tell you of any WG support groups

near you.

A number of groups provide for support and information to vasculitus patients. Many can be found by searching Yahoo and MSN groups. There may be many other listed and major donor supported groups that don't appear on searches. To access email groups on Yahoo, go to http://health.dir.groups.yahoo.com/dir/Health___Wellness   Search for the particular group subject. When the search results come up, sign in if you have not already done so, then click on the name of the one you want. When the group page comes up, click on "Join This Group".
Some of the many WG email groups on Yahoo are:
- Wegener (French)
- Wgdiscussion
- FamilysupportforWegeners (little used)
- Parents4wegeners
- Wegeners-teens-only
- Wegeners4weightloss (little used)
- Wegener's Granulomatosis (VCRC sponsored)
- Wegener's Disease (Europeans only)

In 2010, there will be a Vasculitus Symposium in Long Beach, CA. If you are able to attend, you would have a chance to meet other WG patients, to hear and question leading WG experts, and eat and drink too much (a danger with all medical meetings). For information, see http://www.vasculitisfoundation.org/2010vasculitis-symposium

WHAT ABOUT WEGENER'S?

As you may know, getting diagnosed is often the hardest part of having WG.

And as you may know, WG is chronic and incurable (excepting perhaps by a very risky and expensive process called stem cell transplant). Consequently, a WG patient has to be followed for the remainder of his/her life, with periodic blood, urine, and imaging tests.

As the details of the mechanisms of WG remain incomplete, it is not possible to know exactly what triggers a relapse. Relapses are always possible, and often seem to be triggered by exceptional physical or emotional stress, or sometimes perhaps by infection. Remission of WG can last years, months, or weeks. A few lucky ones never seem to have a relapse.

It is only natural to feel frightened and perhaps despondent because of the damage WG has done or might do. Over time, WG patients find that their spirits improve and the disease is not so scary. Most WG patients get the disease to go into remission and go on to live satisfactory lives, even if not exactly as before.

A positive attitude can be of great help in adjusting to having a chronic disease. Some patients find antidepressants to be useful.

WHAT'S THE FUTURE?
The outcome depends on how much damage the disease has done and whether early and aggressive treatment prevents further damage.

Every possibility one can imagine has happened to WG patients. Some adults take early retirement. Some get less demanding jobs or switch to part time. A few are able to continue working full time - but not many until after successful treatment. Some find their spouses leave. A few have gone to live with relatives to reduce costs etc., etc.

Children may have to be home-schooled or receive specialized instruction and tutoring. College students may have to skip a term or reduce their workload, or drop out for a time.

CLINICAL TRIAL
WG patients can register at the Vasculitus Clinical Research Consortium (VCRC) web page at http://www.rarediseasesnetwork.org/vcrc/ The VCRC is a project of the National Institutes of Health. The VCRC was formed in January 2005 and they are conducting long term "longitudinal" trials as well as gathering detailed information from patients to enable the researchers to develop better means of diagnosing and determining the level of WG activity.

GETTING DIAGNOSED
Unfortunately, most physicians (including ENTs and rheumatologists) have never seen a case of WG so finding the right rheumatologist (or appropriate specialist) is vital.

It is best to be treated by a rheumatologist who has lots of experience treating autoimmune vasculitus. If you cannot find such a one locally, try a major medical centre or teaching hospital. The VF consultants can consult (at no cost) with any physician treating WG, so your physician has more expertise available if needed at http://www.vasculitisfoundation.org/node/44

SOME THINGS TO KNOW

Before treatment for WG, patients should be tested for Alpha-1 Antitrypsin Deficiency (AATD) as it is found in about 8% of WG patients and may require Alpha 1 replacement therapy to avoid liver and lung damage. If this has not been done, the patient should ask his/her physician about ordering the test.

As lungs and kidneys can have significant damage without overt symptoms, it is necessary for WG patients to be closely monitored for changes in those organ functions. CT scans can pick up lung abnormalities that x-rays miss. MRIs are better for soft tissues than CT scans. The 'fifteen-slice' MRI is preferable to one doing fewer slices.

Kidneys can fail rather quickly at times, so while WG is active, a frequent urinalysis including urine creatinine, protein, and blood levels, and for red cell casts is appropriate to make sure no kidney damage is occurring or to assess improvements in functions.

Weekly, or bi-weekly, blood and urine tests you may be receiving at the start of treatment should continue until your disease is in remission. It is generally recommended that a WG patient test their urine even after the disease is in remission to make sure that silent kidney damage is not occurring. Inexpensive urine dipsticks are suitable for that.

You should know that WG can affect virtually any organ in the body. A significant percentage of WG patients have "silent" heart damage, so it is reasonable to have your heart checked for damage caused by WG.

SOME SUGGESTIONS

If you have not already, I suggest you now start a journal, noting symptoms, medications, copies of lab and imaging test results, appointment schedules, questions for your physicians, and answers to those questions, etc. Over time, this will be valuable to you as details are easily forgotten. Write up a medical history that shows all major illnesses and surgeries.

Always prepare for appointments by preparing a list of questions and concerns. Ask your physician for copies of his report after each appointment.

Every interaction with your physician(s) should have an advocate in attendance to take notes and ask questions not thought of earlier. Physicians tend to spend more time and be more thorough when an advocate is present. Your advocate can be a family member or friend who helps you by discussions of treatment options and other aspects of your treatment.

TREATMENT

For rapid reduction of inflammation due to WG, very seriously-ill WG patients may require plasmapheresis in one or more of a series of treatments. It's very important that a person be tested for Alpha 1 Antitrypsin Deficiency (AATD) before receiving plasmapheresis. Some seriously-ill WG patients have responded well to intravenous immunoglobulin G (IVIg).

Most WG patients are treated with Prednisone and Cytoxan (or other corticosteroids and immunosuppressives). Recently, physicians have realized that vasculitus such as WG can cause blood clots so many patients are put permanently on a daily aspirin. A strong immunosuppressive drug such as Cytoxan is usually needed for some time. Prednisone alone rarely gets the disease into remission. Alternative immunosuppressives may be effective. Sometimes only Cytoxan will be effective and must be used. Where major organs are threatened, Cytoxan is commonly required. If you are put on immunosuppressive medications, you will need frequent blood tests to make sure that your white cell count has not dropped too low.

Unfortunately, used in the dosages and durations required, Cytoxan and alternative immunosuppressives may cause female infertility. Women may want to discuss ways of preserving fertility with their physician before starting treatment. Before starting Cytoxan, females can have eggs frozen, or a section of ovary tissue taken for later replacement or there may be other methods to guard against infertility. Male fertility may be affected, but may recover sometime after Cytoxan is stopped.

Parents of children and also young adults may need to discuss with an endocrinologist, possible infertility effects of medications used to treat WG.

There is a recent biological medication called Rituxan (Rituximab). It is expensive but has proved effective where conventional therapies have failed. It probably does not affect fertility. There is a clinical trial, RAVE, using Rituxan to treat WG. Dr. Specks at Mayo Clinic, Rochester, Minnesota has treated some WG patients using Rituxan with good success.

THEY JUST DONOT UNDERSTAND

It is good if your family and friends are supportive as this makes the trip back to health so much easier. However, they may not understand you are ill because WG patients often do not appear ill. Patients on prednisone often gain considerable weight which can sometimes lead to awkward questions.

People on medication used to treat WG can be very moody or irritable. It takes some time and learning on the part of friends and family to realize that you do not have complete control of your emotions while on these drugs.

Sleep-aids sometimes help to get a good night's rest so that one is not completely worn out the next day.

WARNING IF ON PREDNISONE OR A SIMILAR STEROID

If on Prednisone (or similar), then you probably should be on a calcium supplement (1200-1500 mg/day), extra vitamin D3 (400-1000 units/day), and an osteoporosis prevention medication such as Fosamax, Aldronate, Boniva or similar. Those on a bi-phosphonate may be subject to a rare jaw necrosis. If you are not on those supplements but are taking Prednisone, ask your physician about the need for those. (Apparently, children should not be on a biphosphonate).

Prednisone can cause glaucoma, so periodic measurements of internal eye pressure are required to track that. Also, ask your physician about the use of Bactrim DS tablets for prevention of Pneumocystis pneumonia (PCP) and because it may be helpful in preventing relapses. It is prescribed in dosages varying from three tablets per week up to two tablets per day.

MORE BUMPS IN THE ROAD

Some WG patients find they have little trouble with their sinuses. Some find they need to do nasal irrigation to keep things clear. If let go, sinus inflammation can do serious damage. Once the disease is in remission, surgery can correct the "saddle-nose deformity" if that occurs, but, generally, sinus surgery is avoided while the disease is active.

Most WG patients find they do not require pain control once the disease is under control, though if damage has been severe, then pain medications may be required. An endoscopic exam by an ENT who knows what to look for can detect sub-glottal stenosis (narrowing of the trachea) or other throat abnormalities that might be involved in shortness of breath.

Information 2019

[11.9.2019]

I have now been able put the information that has been made available to the public on the internet. Here, I give an overview of the changes since 2010. For me, there seemed a big gap during 2010 to 2017. I did not focus on the matter, the reason being that I wanted to keep a positive mind. Since finding out that I had been given the all-clear, I made a point not too think too much or commit myself in keeping track of the advancements, not until I had to check for any changes in order to progress in the completion of this book.

I still have not consulted any professionals and have purposely left it that way. This book is purely my 'take' on the matter. I offer my journey so that all readers can use this as an alternative source for this matter and use it as they wish. All people are different and will have circumstances that dictate their individual view and journey.

There was some instrumental information that I discovered that would have prepared me for living a better life, such as the blood grouping, essentially my blueprint for living! This information made me re-look at how I have lived my life and how I would have been if I had known and used it earlier in my life, in what to do, what not to do, what to eat, exercise, work, job and so on.

Vasculitus | Doctor | Patient
patient.info/doctor/vasculitus
Vasculitus is a term used to describe a series of conditions in which there is inflammation of the blood vessels. Vasculitus can be primary (occurring on its own), or ...

Vasculitus - NHS
www.nhs.uk/conditions/vasculitis
Vasculitus can range from a minor problem that just affects the skin, to a more serious illness that causes problems with organs like the heart or kidneys. There are many types of vasculitus. The rest of this page discusses a range of potential causes.

Diseases and Conditions Vasculitus - rheumatology.org
www.rheumatology.org/I-Am-A/Patient-Caregiver/...
Physicians suspect vasculitus when a patient has symptoms and abnormal results of the physical examination, laboratory tests or both and there is no other clear cause.

Vasculitus Patient Information | Rare Renal
rarerenal.org/patient-information/vasculitis...
Information about Vasculitus is provided by the Vasculitus RDG and produced
by Vasculitus UK, a registered charity leading support for Vasculitus patients in
the UK.

Vasculitus - Northern Devon Healthcare NHS Trust
www.northdevonhealth.nhs.uk/.../vasculitus
About vasculitus – useful information for vasculitus patients and their carers
Living with vasculitus – more information including benefits, personal stories
and working with vasculitus Arthritis Research UK

Patient Stories - Vasculitus Foundation
www.vasculitisfoundation.org/extraordinary-patients
The VF is the leading organization in the world dedicated to diagnosing, treating,
and curing all forms of vasculitus. The Vasculitus Foundation is a registered
501(c ...

Vasculitus | National Kidney Federation
www.kidney.org.uk/vasculitis
Vasculitus with kidney involvement affects 20-30 people per million population
per year. The trigger that starts vasculitus varies from person to person.
Sometimes it is a 'flu-like infection', sometimes it appears to be a bacterial
infection.

Frequently Asked Vasculitus Questions - Vasculitus UK
www.vasculitis.org.uk/about-vasculitis/frequently-asked...
Forty of the most common questions asked by newly-
diagnosed vasculitus patients including: what is vasculitus, what drugs are used,
is vasculitus hereditary etc.

Vasculitus UK - The UK's Leading Vasculitus Charity
www.vasculitis.org.uk
Welcome to Vasculitus UK Whether you are a patient, carer or medical
professional you will find a wealth of accurate and up-to-date information here,
all derived from ...

Information 2017

If you have vasculitus, you are not alone. There is a strong community of patients and physicians to support you.

Vasculitus Foundation (USA) – www.vasculitisfoundation.org
Vasculitus UK – www.vasculitis.org.uk/
Vasculitus Foundation Canada – www.vasculitis.ca/
American Behcet's Disease Association
Churg-Strauss Syndrome Association
Cryoglobulinemia Home Page
Arthritis Foundation
The American College of Rheumatology
European Vasculitus Study Group: EUVAS Homepage

http://www.wegenersdisease.co.uk

https://www.nhs.uk/conditions/granulomatosis-with-polyangiitis/

In Bangladesh

http://whereindoctor.blogspot.co.uk/p/rheumatology-specialist-doctor-list-of.html
Dr Minhaj Rahman Chowdhury, MMBS, FCPS, MD, DTCD, FACR (USA)
Rheumatologist - Bangabandu Sheik Mujib Medical University
Operates from Japan Bangladesh Friendship Hospital
Address: 55 Satmasjid Road, Zigatola Bus Stand) Dhaka - 1209 Bangladesh
Phone+880-2-9672277
https://www.platform-med.org/blog/2014/12/14/rheumatologists-in-bangladesh/
https://www.facebook.com/lupus.org.bd/posts/608302059226483
http://www.jbfh.org.bd/index.php/component/adsmanager/17-rheumatologist-chest-specialis?Itemid=580
http://www.amarphonebook.com/details/Dhaka/Dr-Minhaj-Rahim-Chowdhury/1/29623
http://www.apollodhaka.com/rheumatology-4/
Bangladesh: Vasculitus department, Birdem, Shahbagh, Dhaka
Bangladesh: Bangabandu Sheikh Mujib Medical University

List of Drugs and Side Effects

http://www.vasculitis.org.uk/about-vasculitis/glossary-of-drugs

Steroids and Immunosuppressants

Both Prednisalone (steroids) and Immunosuppressants such as Cyclophosphamide, Azathioprine, Methotrexate and Mycophenolate Mofetil reduce inflammation by suppressing the activity of the white blood cells. However, by doing this these white blood cells are less able to fight infection. The immunosuppressants can also suppress the production of cells from the bone marrow.

If necessary, blood tests will be performed to monitor closely the white blood count and haemoglobin (to detect anaemia). If a patient has signs of a fever or infection, it is imperative that they seek medical attention.

Not all the side effects noted with these drugs are mentioned below. Patients are advised to read the patient leaflet supplied with the drugs, and speak to their physician/pharmacist if they are unsure about anything contained in the leaflet.

Vasculitus UK recommends the following PDF for information about cortisone (steroids) and corticosteroid therapies: <u>Cortisone-info</u> The PDF contains a wealth of information from side effects, to steroid reduction and everything between.

List of drugs and side effects used in the treatment of vasculitus

The following is a list of many of the drugs used to treat and maintain remission in the various vasculitides. Some of the drugs mentioned are prophylactic (prescribed to prevent disease). A number of the drugs are general to many of the vasculitides whilst others are specific to individual vasculitic diseases.

The list is not exhaustive and new drugs are constantly being developed. The lists of side effects is not exhaustive and patients are encouraged to read the information sheets supplied with prescription medication and to discuss any concerns with their medical team.

Adalimumab (Humira)

This is an artificially-manufactured antibody that can be injected to reduce the effect of tumour necrosis factor alpha (TNF). TNF is an important protein in the body that can cause inflammation and is important in fighting infection. Immediate side-effects are unusual but can include: mouth ulceration, diarrhoea, coughing, dizziness, fatigue, paraesthesia (tingling of the skin), musculoskeletal pain, rash and pruritus (itching). A major side-effect can be a reduced ability to fight some types of infection and possibly to control cancer cells in the body.

Antihistamines
These are used to treat allergies and itching. Sedating anti-histamines may initially cause sleepiness. Non-sedating anti-histamines rarely cause drowsiness.

Azathioprine (Imuran)
This is an important and very commonly-used immunosuppressant. Major side-effects are unusual but blood tests must be carried out frequently when it is started or the dose is increased, because there is a risk of liver toxicity and bone marrow suppression (low white cell count and anaemia). Other side-effects include fatigue, hair loss, diarrhoea, and increased risk of infection.

Bactrim (see Co-trimoxazole)

Biphosphonate (including Zolidronic acid, Risedronate and others)
A major side effect of long term prednisolone-use is osteoporosis. Biphosphonate may be prescribed to strengthen bones and help prevent osteoporosis. Side-effects from oral biphosphonate are usually mild but include nausea, dyspepsia, diarrhoea or constipation and headaches. They cannot be used in patients with marked kidney damage.

Cellcept (see Mycophenolate Mofetil)

Cyclosporine
This is an immunosuppressant which works by reducing the function of the lymphocytes (a type of white cell). In the long term, it can cause chronic damage to the kidneys and this should be carefully monitored. In high doses, it can cause reversible problems to the kidney or liver function and cause paraesthesia (tingling in hands and feet), fatigue and headache.

Colchicines
Colchicine is an anti-inflammatory drug commonly used to treat attacks of gout. It is also sometimes used to treat some forms of vasculitus such as Behcet's disease and hypersensitivity vasculitus. It is usually given in a tablet form and often only for short periods. Common side-effects are nausea, vomiting and abdominal pain. Patients with impaired kidney function may not be able to remove the drug properly from the body and should be prescribed in short courses, only. It rarely causes damage to kidneys, liver, nerves and muscles. Long-term use should only be under expert supervision.

Cortisone (see Steroids)

Co-trimoxazole or Septrin (Bactrim)
This is an antibiotic prescribed to some patients being treated with high doses of an immunosuppressant to prevent the lung infection, Pneumocystis carinii (also known as Pneumocystis jerovicii) pneumonia. It is also sometimes used in patients with Wegener's Granulomatosis (Granulomatosis with polyangiitis) as it may reduce the risk of relapse in some patients. Side-effects include: nausea, diarrhoea, headache, a rash and, more rarely, a low white cell count.

Cox 2 inhibitors (See Non-steroidal anti-inflammatory drugs)

Cyclophosphamide
Cyclophosphamide is commonly used to treat severe forms of vasculitis and is also widely known as an anti-cancer chemotherapy drug. It is usually given as either a daily tablet or an intermittent injection every few weeks.

Cyclophosphamide has the potential to cause serious short term side-effects including bladder irritation (cystitis) and bone marrow suppression (low white cell count) leading to infection. Mesna (a uroprotectant) is often given to patients receiving injections of Cyclophosphamide to reduce the risk of bladder problems. Patients may also be advised to drink a lot of water to flush out the bladder but this should be discussed with the medical practitioner. Other short-term effects include nausea, vomiting and hair loss.

Over a longer period of time, Cyclophosphamide can cause infertility in both men and women. Men who may still want to have children should, therefore, consider sperm banking.

Long term use of Cyclophosphamide is considered undesirable and has been linked to an increased risk of some types of cancer, e.g. cancer of the bladder.

Cytoxan (see Cyclophosphamide)

Dapsone
Dapsone is an antibiotic which is sometimes used to control vasculitus limited to the skin (neutrophilic dermatoses). It can cause nausea, dizziness, headache and insomnia.

Dexamethasone (See Steroids)

Etanercept
This is an artificially-manufactured protein that can be injected to reduce the effect of tumour necrosis factor alpha (TNF). TNF is an important protein in the body that can cause inflammation and is important in fighting infection. Immediate side-effects are unusual but can include: dyspnoea (shortness of breath), confusion, paraesthesia (tingling of the skin) and vertigo. A major side effect can be a reduced ability to fight some types of infection and possibly to control cancer cells in the body.

Humira (see Adalimumab)

Immunoglobulin
Normal human immunoglobulin is sometimes used to treat some forms of vasculitus, often when other treatments cannot be tolerated or have been ineffective. It is a particularly important treatment in Kawasaki's Disease. It is given as an intravenous infusion and repeated infusions may be necessary. Side-effects are common during or following each infusion including nausea, diarrhoea, chills, fever, headache, dizziness, joint, muscle and back pains. In rare cases, it may cause serious allergic reactions or kidney failure.

Imuran (See Azathioprine)

Infliximab
This is an artificially-manufactured antibody that can be injected to reduce the effect of tumour necrosis factor alpha (TNF). TNF is an important protein in the body that can cause inflammation and is important in fighting infection. Immediate side-effects are unusual but can include: diarrhoea, flushing, chest pain, dyspnoea (shortness of breath), dizziness and fatigue. A major side-effect can be a reduced ability to fight some types of infection and possibly to control cancer cells in the body.

Lansoprazole
Used to treat and prevent damage caused by the use of NSAIDs. (see NSAIDs)

Losec (see Omeprazole)

Mesna
Mesna is an "uroprotectant" used to prevent bladder damage during intermittent cyclophosphamide treatment. Side-effects include: nausea, diarrhoea, headache, a rash or dizziness.

Methotrexate
This is an important and very commonly-used immunosuppressant. Major side-effects are unusual but blood tests must be carried out frequently when it is started or as the dose is increased because there is a risk of liver toxicity and bone marrow suppression (low white cell count and anaemia). Patients should also be aware that methotrexate can cause both short and long-term lung damage which should be monitored. Other side-effects include: gastro-intestinal (GI) upset, dyspepsia (indigestion), dizziness, fatigue, chills, headaches and mood changes.

Methylprednisolone (See Steroids)

Monoclonal antibodies
These include Adalimumab (Humira), Infliximab and Rituximab

Mycophenolate Mofetil (Cellcept) and Mycophenolic acid (Myfortic)
This drug is an important and quite commonly-used immunosuppressant. Major side-effects are unusual but blood tests must be carried out frequently when it is started or as the dose is increased because there is a risk of bone marrow suppression (low white cell count and anaemia). Side-effects include: diarrhoea, vomiting, dyspnoea (shortness of breath), insomnia, skin irritation and flu-like symptoms. Stomach and bowel side effects are also relatively common.

Mycophenolic acid (see Mycophenolate Mofetil)

Myfortic (see Mycophenolate Mofetil)

Non-steroidal anti-inflammatory drugs[(NSAIDs) and Cox 2 inhibitors]
This group of drugs includes ibuprofen, diclofenac (voltarol) indomethacin, celecoxib and etoricoxib. They are commonly prescribed for the control of pain, especially joint pain and can be very effective. Some of them are available without prescription. However, they should be used with caution as they commonly have side-effects and can interfere with other prescribed medication. Even the drugs available without prescription can cause problems and patients should discuss with their medical practitioner before taking them.

Side-effects are common with these drugs. Serious side-effects include the risk of stomach ulcers and bleeding ulcers; an increase in the overall risk of bleeding and an increase in the risk of heart attacks and strokes. These drugs can also cause serious problems for patients with any form of kidney disease and they should not be taken by patients with this kind of problem without careful discussion with the medical practitioner. They should also not be taken by patients with a history of stomach ulcers. They can also cause problems with fluid retention and high blood pressure.

NSaids (see Non-steroidal anti-inflammatory drugs)

Omeprazole
Used to treat and protect damage caused by the use of NSaids (see NSaids)

Prednisalone (see Steroids)

Prednisone (see Steroids)

Ranitidine
Used to treat and prevent damage caused by the use of NSaids. (see NSaids)

Risedronate (see Bisphosphonates)

Rituximab
This is an artificially-manufactured antibody which removes B-cells (a type of white cell). It is now increasingly being used in patients as an alternative to cyclophosphamide and other immunosuppressants in the types of vasculitus where B cells and the antibodies they produce are thought to be important. Side-effects are generally mild and are infusion-related - occurring during or up to two hours after infusion. Side-effects include: rashes and gastro-intestinal (GI) upset.

Septrin (see Co-trimoxazole)

Steroids (Prednisolone, Methylprednisolone, Cortisone, Prednisone, Dexamethasone)

Steroids are naturally-occurring hormones produced in the body by the adrenal glands and are essential for normal health. Artificial steroids are commonly used to treat vasculitus and other inflammatory diseases and are very effective at reducing inflammation. They are often used initially at high doses to control the disease and then lowered as quickly as is possible to reduce the side-effects.

Unfortunately, side-effects are very common with steroid medication. Common serious side-effects include increased risk of infection, diabetes and osteoporosis. Other common side-effects include weight gain, disturbed sleep, altered mood (including on rare occasion, depression and very rarely, psychosis), muscle weakness, dyspepsia (indigestion) and stomach ulcers; increased hair growth, fluid retention, increased blood pressure and thin skin.

When artificial steroids are being taken, the adrenal glands may stop producing the body's own steroids, so it is essential that the patient does not stop taking steroids suddenly as this may lead to a steroid deficiency which could cause significant problems. The rate of reduction must, therefore, be closely monitored by the physician.

It is essential that patients on a high dosage of steroids are monitored for the development of diabetes. If appropriate, patients may be prescribed bisphosphonates, calcium or vitamin D to protect their bones. Patients may also be prescribed tablets to protect the stomach from side-effects (e.g. Ranitidine, Lansoprazole, Omeprazole or similar).

Further in-depth information on steroids, for patients and their family, is available at: Cortisone Information

Tacrolimus - Similar to Ciclosporin
This is an immunosuppressant which works by reducing the function of lymphocytes (a type of white cell). Side-effects can include: headache, diarrhoea, nausea, blurred vision and constipation.

Zantac (see Ranitidine)

Zoldronic acid (see Bisphosphonates)

The Books

1.

As well as the website which covers many of the Saints, Phirs and Fakirs, the following books focus on the main Saint of Sylhet. Hazrat Shah Jalal was the leader of the group which consisted of three hundred and sixty, or so, companions.

The five books cover much of Hazrat Shahjalal's life and the customs of today which his companions' lineage still follows and service.

2.

- 1. The white book is about Hazrat Shahjalal.

- 2. The blue book is about his burial place.

- 3. The black book is about the tradition that starts the process of his commemoration.

- 4. The pink book is about a custom that is inherent and intrinsic to the commemoration.

3.

- 5. The yellow book is the commemoration capturing the procession and the pageantry.

Hazrat Shahjalal is revered by the locals as well as people of every caste and religion.

There is historical evidence of the Officers of the British Empire paying homage there before beginning their time in office.

4.

Many couples come to the shrine and pay homage for good health, life and their children.

5.

And, of course, I went there for my health and here I am, seven years on, writing about the experience and living a disease-free life.

If you would like to read and learn about Hazrat Shah Jalal or want to pay a visit then check the books out in the catalogue section and/or email me.

How I managed?

I have been through everything that I have written in this book. As you will note, there are many things that happened without me knowing about it and many are part and parcel of living this trip and completing the journeys within it.

I knew that I needed to off-load all my anxieties and stresses as well as the hurt and pain that were lodged inside of me.

How long since I have been C & P ANCA free? I have been free from it since 19th May 2010. This information came from a test done in Bangladesh. Although I had this information, I was still not comfortable and sure about it until I had come back to London and had a further test there, which confirmed it.

I was diagnosed with the disease in December 2009.In May 2010, I had the negative report from the hospital in Dhaka, Bangladesh which was confirmed for me in the UK in 2011.

At that time in 2009, the life span was four to five years. 2016 would have been my five year stretch and that was always in the back of my mind after I had been given the 'all-clear' in London in 2011. I was, in effect, 'holding on' to see if I would make it past 2016.Since I started writing this book in 2017, so much has changed but today, in 2020, I am still here, alive and WG/P free.

Glossary

Words & Phrases	Translation
Akri	Final
Amanullah	A name
Auwliyah	Saints
Bangabandu Sheik Mujib	Name of the first Prime minister of Bangladesh
Bedeshi	Foreigners
Dhaka	Name of the capital city of Bangladesh
Dorga	Shrine
Fajar Namaz	Dawn prayers
Fakir	Vagabond
Gilaf	Material covering
Hazrat	A title, honourable
Kobir Ahmed	Name
Lakri Tura	A event name:
Londoni	Term used by Bangladeshi natives to refer to Bangladeshi who reside in London
Makkah	Name of the place in Saudi Arabia where muslims travel to do pilgrimage
Mazar Sharif	Mausoleum
Mehendi	Name of the plant that stains the skin orange when applied
Milad	Gathering
Minhaj Rahman Chowdhury	Name of the Rheumatology doctor I consulted in Dhaka, the capitol city of Bangladesh.
Mohilia shag	Green leafy plant
Moulivi Bazaar	Name of a town, in the district of Sylhet, A division in Bangladesh
Moutowalli	A title:
Mukam	Shrine
Namaz	Prayers
NRB	Non Resident Bangladeshi
Phagoleh doriliseh	A phrase: possessed
Phirs	Hermit / shaman

Probashi	Non Resident Bangladeshi
Satmasjid Road	A name of a road in Dhaka, capitol city of Bangladesh
Shah	A title:
Shah Jalal	Name of the Sufi saint of Sylhet, Bangladesh
Shah Mullah Mubarak Shahab	Name of a Sufi saint from my father's side
Shah Sikondor Shahab	Name of a Sufi saint from my mother's side
Shahab	A Title:
Sylhet	Name of a town in the district of Sylhet, Bangladesh
Urus	An event: veneration of a saint
W. G	Stands for Wegener's Granulomatosis
Zigatola	A name of a road in Dhaka, capital city of Bangladesh

Bibliography

1. Healing Journey" by Matthew Manning
2. Eat Right for Your Type, By Dr Peter J. D'Adamo with Catherine Whitney, Putnum, USA, 1996
3. Mazaar Sharif, By Mayar Akash, MAPublisher, UK, 2017
4. Urus Commemoration, by Mayar Akash, MAPublisher, UK. 2017
5. Lakri Tura, by Mayar Akash, MAPublisher, UK, 2017
6. Gilaf Procession, by Mayar Akash, MAPublisher, UK, 2016
7. Shah Jalal, by Mayar Akash, MAPublisher, UK, 2017
8. The Complete Master Key System, by Charles Haanel, BN Publishing, USA, 2010
9. Personality Types, by Elizabeth Puttick, Hay House, UK, 2009

Reference

Websites:

http://www.vasculitis-patient.com/Anti-Inflammatory_Foods.html

http://www.vasculitis-patient.com/7_medical_tests.php#Dipsticks

http://www.vasculitis-patient.com/14_nasal_dental_diet.php#Food

http://www.ucl.ac.uk/ioo/pdf/PI/Professor%20Sue%20Lightman.pdf

http://www.vasculitis-patient.com

http://www.vasculitisfoundation.org

http://www.vasculitisfoundation.org/2010vasculitis-symposium

http://rarediseasesnetwork.epi.usf.edu/vcrc/index.htm

http://vasculitisfoundation.org

http://www.vasculitisfoundation.org/support/domestication.org/node/1921

http://www.vasculitisfoundation.org/support/international

http://health.dir.groups.yahoo.com/dir/Health___Wellness

http://www.rarediseasesnetwork.org/vcrc/

http://www.vasculitisfoundation.org/node/44

http://www.nytimes.com/1995/09/15/us/scientists-discover-gene-that-causes-inflammation.html

https://www.youtube.com/watch?v=ReRcHdeUG9Y&t=1173s [22.11.19]

https://www.bilogistik.com/en/blog/lng-cng-lpg-road-transport/[9.7.2020]

http://theamericanswillcome.blogspot.com/2013/03/the-auto-rickshaws-cng.html[9.7.2020]

https://www.daily-sun.com/post/113320/Japan-Bangladesh-Friendship-Hospital-fined-for-irregularities[9.7.2020]

https://www.birdembd.org/[9.7.2020]

https://www.ucanews.com/news/government-gets-tough-on-low-grade-pharmaceuticals/50488[9.7.2020]

https://www.youtube.com/watch?reload=9&v=eqT8AK_6-DU[11.7.2020]

https://iccia.com/?q=islamicTourism/airports&ctr=Bangladesh[11.7.2020]

https://www.facebook.com/BBCOne/videos/277346466911012[23-7-2020]

https://www.facebook.com/photo?fbid=10164555417810268&set=gm.659651544958690[30-8-2020]

The above list was the information available to me at the time of writing this book but things may have changed and progressed a lot since then.

NB: *Please note that the information in the email section was written in 2010 and may be out of date. Please check all links and information for updates on-line. Knowledge about Wegener's Granulomatosis is always being discovered.

MAPublisher Catalogue

ISBN/Titles /Image/Author	ISBN/Titles /Image/Author	ISBN/Titles /Image/Author	ISBN/Titles /Image/Author
978-1-910499-00-9 Father to child By Mayar Akash	978-1-910499-08-5 HSJ Lakri Tura By Mayar Akash	978-1-910499-26-9 Colouring 1-10 By MAPublisher	978-1-910499-18-4 Basic Numbers 1-10 By MAPublisher
978-1-910499-16-0 River of Life By Mayar Akash	978-1-910499-09-2 HSJ Gilaf Procession By Mayar Akash	978-1-910499-27-6 Activity Numbers 1-10 By MAPublisher	978-1-910499-19-1 Number 1-100 By MAPublisher
978-1-910499-39-9 Eyewithin By Mayar Akash	978-1-910499-03-0 HSJ Mazar Sharif By Mayar Akash	978-1-910499-28-3 Activity Colouring Alphabets By MAPublisher	978-1-910499-20-7 Vowels By MAPublisher
978-1-910499-32-0 WG Survivor By Mayar Akash	978-1-910499-06-1 Hazrat Shahjalal By Mayar Akash	978-1-910499-68-9 The Adventures of Sylheti mazars By Mayar Akash	978-1-910499-21-4 Alphabet Consonants By MAPublisher
978-1-910499-66-5 Yesteryears By Mayar Akash	978-1-910499-07-8 HSJ Urus By Mayar Akash	978-1-910499-38-2 Bite Size Islam: 99 Names of Allah By Mayar Akash	978-1-910499-22-1 Vowels & Short By MAPublisher

ISBN/Titles /Image/Author	ISBN/Titles /Image/Author	ISBN/Titles /Image/Author	ISBN/Titles /Image/Author
978-1-910499-15-3 Anthology One By Penny Authors	978-1-910499-36-8 Delirious By Liam Newton	978-1-910499-52-8 Lit From Within By Ruth Lewarne	978-1-910499-57-3 The Vampire of the Resistance By Ruth Lewarne
978-1-910499-17-7 Anthology Two By Penny Authors	978-1-910499-54-2 Book of Lived v6 Penny Authors	978-1-910499-49-8 Cry for Help By B. M. Gandhi	978-1-910499-55-9 Riversolde By Meriyon
978-1-910499-29-0 Book of Lived v3 By Penny Authors	978-1-910499-37-5 When You Look Back By Rashma Mehta	978-1-910499-14-6 The Halloweeen Poem by Zainab Khan	978-1-910499-70-2 Smiley & The Acorn By Roger Underwood
978-1-910499-351 V4 Book of Lived By Penny Authors	978-1-910499-37-5 My Dream World By Rashma Mehta	978-1-910499-69-6 Consciousness By Mustak Mustafa	978-1-910499-40-5 World's First University By Giasuddin Ahmed
978-1-910499-50-4 Book of Lived v5 By Penny Authors	978-1-910499-53-5 Angel Eyez By Rashma Mehta	978-1-910499-73-3 Book of Lived v7 By Penny Authors	978-1-910499-56-6 The Warrior Queen By Giasuddin Ahmed

All books are available on-line,
https://www.waterstones.com/author/mayar-akash/1973183 [3.3.23]

ISBN/Titles /Image/Author	ISBN/Titles /Image/Author	ISBN/Titles /Image/Author	ISBN/Titles /Image/Author
978-1-910499-58-0 EEP:Tower Hamlets, Random, One Mayar Akash	978-1-910499-60-3 EEP:Tower Hamlets, Random, Two By Mayar Akash	978-1-910499-05-4 Tide of Change By Mayar Akash	978-1-910499-51-1 Brick & Mortar By Mayar Akash
978-1-910499-61-0 Grenfell Tower By Mayar Akash	978-1-910499-63-4 EEP: Power Houses, Clove Crescent By Mayar Akash	978-1-910499-71-9 Altab Ali Murder By Mayar Akash	978-1-910499-31-3 Pathfinders By Mayar Akash
978-1-910499-62-7 EEP: Community Service 1992-1993 By Mayar Akash	978-1-910499-64-1 EEP:Bancroft Estate By Mayar Akash	978-1-910499-11-5 Re-Awakening By Mayar Akash	978-1-910499-13-9 Chronicle of Sylhetis of UK By Mayar Akash
978-1-910499-59-7 EEP:Brick Lane, Spitalfields By Mayar Akash	978-1-910499-72-6 25th Anniversary of Bangladesh By Mayar Akash	978-1-910499-12-2 Young Voice Mayar Akash	978-1-910499-42-9 Bangladeshi Fishes By Mayar Akash
978-1-910499-65-8 PYO Polish Exchange 1992 By Mayar Akash	978-1-910499-30-6 TH Bangladeshi Politicians By Mayar Akash	978-1-910499-10-8 Vigil Subotaged By Mayar Akash	978-1-910499-67-2 F. Ahmed and History By Mukid Choudhury

All books are available on-line, Google the titles and they will take you to the sites where you can acquire copies.

ISBN/Titles /Image/Author	ISBN/Titles /Image/Author	ISBN/Titles /Image/Author	ISBN/Titles /Image/Author
978-1-910499-43-6 My Life Book 1 By Mayar Akash	978-1-910499-44-3 My Life Book 2 By Mayar Akash	978-1-910499-45-0 My Life Book 3 By Mayar Akash	978-1-910499-46-7 My Life Book 4 By Mayar Akash
978-1-910499-47-4 My Life Book 5 By Mayar Akash	978-1-910499-75-7 Bangladeshis in Manchester - Oral History, Part 1 By M.A. Mustak	978-1-910499-74-0 Peter Fox Artist By Peter Fox	

All books are available on-line, Google the titles and they will take you to the sites where you can acquire copies.

You will also find the on-line catalogue on the following link.
https://www.lulu.com/spotlight/mayarakash3bb00494 [3.3.2022]

www.ingramcontent.com/pod-product-compliance
Lightning Source LLC
Chambersburg PA
CBHW021504090426
42739CB00007B/466